the ULTIMATE
guide to the *perfect*
Card

prose • sentiments • poems • expressions

BY
LINDA LATOURELLE
AND
CC MILAM

Bluegrass PUBLISHING
www.bluegrasspublishing.com
270.251.3600

For information write:
Bluegrass Publishing, Inc.
PO Box 634
Mayfield, KY 42066 USA
service@bluegrasspublishing.com
www.BluegrassPublishing.com

ISBN: 978-0-9761925-3-4

Mayfield, KY : Bluegrass Publishing, Inc. 2007

Cover Design: Todd Jones, Tennessee
Proudly printed in the United States of America

RECOGNITION

recognition\rec̀og*ni'tion\, n. the process of recognizing something or someone by acknowledging their accomplishments with a show of appreciation for everything they do

To recognize the kindness and help from others is a willful act of appreciation.

> **dedicate**\ded'i*cate\, v. 1. To set apart and consecrate, as to a divinity, or for sacred uses; to devote formally: *"They dedicate their lives to God."*

Dear Lord, It is with adoration and praise that I dedicate this book to you. You have poured out your blessings on it already and it is exciting to be a part of this journey. I know that you have a great purpose here and it is my prayer that if nothing else, one life may be touched by its contents.

This birth of this book is truly awesome. You have put it together with such amazing connections from around this world. Through it you have opened so many doors and blessed in ways inconceivable. Thus, it is with the greatest love that I say Thank You! My fervent prayer is for all that is accomplished as a result of this book to bring awesome Glory to you and a humbleness of spirit to myself and all who read it. I stand in awe of you.   – Linda

Dear Daughters,
You are the light of my life and my greatest blessing in this world. You are so incredibly talented, beautiful and precious. God gave me my heart's desire with your love. May my life be a joyful blessing and encouragement to you everyday of your life. I love you forever and always. May you continue to let your light shine for the Lord. Thank you for all of your help and patience through all of this. I know there will be many blessings for the honor you show me everyday. I love you with all my heart.

Love, Momma

> **kindness**\kind'ness\, n. A kind act; an act of good will;
> as, to do a great kindness; an instance of kind behavior:
> *"I will always remember your many kindnesses to me."*

Todd Jones. If there are miracle makers here on earth–this is the man who can do it! It is with the sincerest gratitude that I tell you how awesome you are. I know that you are instrumental in helping to share the blessings within these pages, because the totally brilliant design work you do adds the intrigue for our readers to open the book. Words such as thank you don't do justice to all you have done for me! You are such a wonderful friend and I truly am honored to know you and Cindy...You are the BEST! I thank the Lord for every remembrance of you–my dear friend!

GG Milam. May you be as blessed and excited as you share your talents with the world. Oh, my–what an awesome job you have done in helping revise (revive) my (our) cardbook! It is so beautiful and you have done an amazing job with it. The attention to detail and creativity that you have given has been great. Thank you for hanging in there. I pray that your life will be blessed by this and that through it, you will come to find a passion in your writing–it is a talent, a gift sent with a special purpose. You're shining dear sister! I Love YOU!

"True kindness is a gift that cannot be given with anything of this world." ~ Linda LaTourelle

> **thanks**\thanks\, pl.n. Grateful feelings or thoughts: gratitude: a heart full of thanks. An expression of gratitude: a note of thanks to a contributor: *"He gave thanks to God."*

Thanks is such a small word when one desires to express tremendous gratitude to special people for their kindness. It is nothing short of a miracle that this book has come together so quickly. But when you have the ULTIMATE Guide that I do, how could I expect anything else. I am blessed by a multitude of friends.

From the writings within, the proof-reading, the typing, the contributions, the prayers and more, God has put together a special collection of thoughts and feelings to enable it's readers to be inspired and take from the pages words that might bless others.

My heartfelt thanks to:

My Girls
My Parents
My Brothers
Jennifer Byerly
Barbara Cox
Marsha Cruse
Sharon Ezzell
Anna Faye
Dee Gruenig
Warren Gruenig
August Jones

Todd Jones
Lottie Ann Knox
The Ladies
Nicole McKinney
GG Milam
Teri Olund
Shanda Purcell
Lynne Rogers
Thena Smith
Holly VanDyne
Linda Zimmerman

No act of kindness, no matter how small, is ever wasted. ~Aesop

Table of Contents

Table of Contents

SENTiMENTS

These are the feelings
deep in my heart, filling my
soul with words to impart.
How do I tell you in
so many ways? I'm sorry,
Congrats, or Hip Hip hooray?
Love that is heartfelt &
romance so rare–
Oh, how many feelings
I am longing to share.
So what's in a word
and where do I start?
With wisdom and love that
comes straight from my heart!
~Linda LaTourelle © 2004

To Thena, my dear sister and friend–
Thanks for the finishing touch!

Going to take
a sentimental journey~

*For I know the plans I have for you...
to give you hope and a future.*
Jeremiah 29:11

The journey of life begins long before birth.
A child is but a whisper in a mother's ear from God
that becomes her heart's desire—just as He first loved us.
With determination and devotion, a mother...
endures the pain and feels the joy to bring us to life.
Her emotions run the gamut as she watches us grow.
On every single step of a child's journey—
with faithfulness and unconditional love,
purpose, patience and prayer,
a mother perseveres all the days of her life.
Her love lives on throughout eternity through each generation.
It is with the utmost love that I dedicate this book
To my dear Mother—

Joyce Ellen Anderson Chapman

Dear

Friend,

This is a subject that has been dear to my heart for years and years. It seems apparent with the way the world is now that too often we neglect the people we love most. We get caught up in day to day living and unfortunately forget that our family needs to hear and see our love. One way you can do this is through writing. Don't think that you can't write, because you know how to talk, thus you can write. Tell them your feelings. All you really need to do is put on to paper what you feel in your heart–simple and sweet! My prayer is that you will make some time soon and sit down to put your love on paper in the form of a journal or a love letter to each member of your family. I have even done circle journaling with my girls, at times, to share our feelings with each other. People don't care how you say it, they just care that you do. If you have children or a parent, take the time now, while you have the time, no matter how young or old your family is and write to them, for them and for you. I promise you that it will be one of the most precious blessings you can give to them. Husband, wife, son, daughter, parent, sister or brother–your gift will be a treasure to them and future generations.

Blessings,
Linda

Cardmaking: Using a piece of cardstock to create a greeting card which has verses to express particular sentiments or feelings by adding embellishments for a special person or occasion

If you can talk you really can write. But now that you have this book, it will most certainly simplify things for you. The words within this book are meant to inspire, uplift and cheer all who peruse it's pages. You can use it to create just about any type of card you find necessary. May it touch your life and the lives of others in a very special way.

~ Linda

Words,

thoughts and heartfelt sentiments are the memories that linger long after the event or occasion. Your love for someone special portrayed in the ink upon the paper by your touch. Oh, what a joy to behold.

Have you ever gone to your mailbox and discovered a handwritten envelope from someone special? It's such a cherished gift, a lasting treasure! What is even better is to open that envelope and discover that someone you know took the time to pen warm, loving sentiments to you. While many people will just write their thoughts within a ready-made card from a store, others will use a blank note card and yet others will give a handmade creation. Whatever the choice, their ultimate desire is to share their heart.

Creating cards are becoming a fast growing hobby, with designer books and magazines specific to the market now available. With scrapbooking so big in the industry, the cardmaking was certain to have a natural following. Add to that, the growth of the rubberstamp companies, and the potential is awe inspiring, limited only by the imagination of the cardmaker.

With the Internet so accessible, e-cards have become one of the preferred methods of communication with family and friends. While convenient to send off a quick e-card or postcard, nothing can replace the loving feeling upon receiving a handmade card. Unfortunately we neglect to do the most simple and meaningful things because of the fast paced life most people live. However, there is nothing that can speak to the heart of your loved ones the way something you have created personally for them can.

In gathering items for my scrapbook albums, one of the most cherished mementos for me to come across is a note or card from someone I love. The ones I hold particularly close are the cards and notes from my children and those from family members no longer with us. When I stop to read a card made in grade school by one of my daughters it brings to me a soul-soothing smile as I reflect upon the fond memories of those earlier days. I find a familiar handwritten letter from my great-grandmother and I think about her loveliness and sweetness. I remember how I miss her and how long ago she went home to be with the Lord. The joy I feel as I read through these precious treasures again and again brings tears of joy and love. What a flood of memories fill my soul as I look at the feelings expressed by my loved ones in these simple sentiments.

I know from personal experience, there are many times in life that finding just the right card is so important. I remember times that an occasion would arise and I could spend an hour or more in the card section of a store or perhaps several stores looking for what I had in mind. There were times it was hard to find that perfect card, too, and even times when I just couldn't. So then it would mean going home and trying to come up with something on my own either on the computer or by creating a handmade card. My children have always made their own cards; they receive a blessing in creating them. It allows them to express their love in an artistic way and that is a joy for them.

CHERISHED MEMENTOS

There are so many wonderful papers, inks and products now on the market, you can embellish your heart out. Making cards is pure delight! Years ago I was involved quite a bit with rubberstamping, but due to many other things there was little time left to really explore the possibilities. I recently went to a craft show and was so impressed with the amazing card creations by some local rubberstampers. Such beauty was in these delicate works of art and then to add to them heartfelt expressions, these cards become irreplaceable pieces that will keep on giving to the recipients for generations to come. Rubberstamping has come a long way in the last twenty years.

With the blending of scrapbooking and rubberstamping, cardmaking is limited only by your imagination. There are many good articles in magazines about cardmaking and even a few books out there about techniques, lots of products, too. Good news, for cardmakers—there is a great new magazine designed specifically for the cardmaker, "Simply Sentiments." More information in the "Resource" section of this book.

Would you like to open your mailbox and find love in a simple envelope? Well, let it start with you and trickle on out. Within this book are words that have come down through the generations. Words that still inspire even now. There are also words from today created with the same passion as those of long ago. And, if you search these pages, you will see more in these perfect words. You will see your words, hidden within this book, hidden within your heart. Words ready to leap off the page or out of your heart to honor another in some particular way.

Trust
your heart! Pray about the occasion for which you need a card. Read the book, search your heart, understand in your mind what it is you want to convey. The words WILL come just believe that sentiments of our heart are often revealed in the quietness of mind and spirit. You will know when the words are right and when they are, there is no gift that can bless more in this incredible way.

So begin today and as you come across places in this book that touch you, highlight them. If you feel they are words relevant to a particular person or situation, make notations. Use this book and allow it to inspire you. I know you will come to a place where you find your words and in doing so your life will be touched.

Here are the feelings
From deep in my heart.
Words from my soul
That I long to impart.
Words of love so heartfelt
That I long to share.
Some read like poetry
Others a prayer...

~ Thena Smith © 2004

Here are some thoughts about cards. When you receive a card do you find it difficult to throw it away? I have a collection of the really special ones from those close to me. The ones I treasure most are those with handwritten sentiments. To me, cards that someone took the time to create and share their heart are the greatest blessings. It's very difficult to throw away something that you know was a gift of love.

I want to take a moment to share about a card that was such a surprise and an amazing blessing. About ten years ago, on our move to Kentucky, my father blew my socks off with his creation given to me on my birthday. Now you see, my dad is a great salesman, golfer, intellectual, but never have I known him as a man with artistic ability of the cardmaking kind. I don't know what inspired him the day he created a handmade masterpiece, but I will treasure it always. He used a manila file folder and covered it with pictures gathered from the beautiful Country magazines and others he found. He wrote in his own hand sentiments that touched my very soul. It was a special blessing. He never liked store bought cards and really wasn't the sentimental type, so he would always encourage my mother to create her own. When my sister, in California, became partners in a scrapbook store she got our mother interested in scrapbooking and eventually creating cards. I am so blessed, because every card she gives now is handmade with her love and artistic ability. It's been a wonderful blessing for her, also, as she creates individual cards for all of her children and grandchildren. I cherish each and every card I have received from her. Now each time I look at these cards and I see her handwriting, I know the love behind it.

When I close my eyes I can picture her in my mind's eye sitting at her table creating these little gems. Such sweet blessings from my mother's heart—Thanks Mom and Dad—you are a treasure!

Now, back to my point, which I guess I just made. Throwing away a handmade card is next to impossible. The recipient will always value the love that went into it. Think about cards your children made when they were little. Did it break your heart to toss it? Or do you tuck them away, like me? Now that you know all this, think of the blessing you are giving with the gift of a handmade card to that someone special. Just like scrapbooking, or any craft for that matter, not everyone is really artistically inclined or wants to be. But in cardmaking, things are a bit different. Cards can be created using the simplest of tools and designs. You are only limited by your imagination.

Imagination is the soul within
~ Linda LaTourelle

Imagination? You say that you don't have one? (or at least you think you don't!) No more excuses—with cardmaking you can K.I.S.S. (keep it simple...) The design on your card can be created in a matter of seconds with a few rubber stamps, your computer or you can utilize the techniques available through many sources now on the market. There are some lovely full color books out there about cardmaking techniques that will teach you step by step. A new website to visit for cardmakers is www.simplysentiments.com. Just go to your local scrapbook or rubberstamp store and ask for books and magazines or classes that are specific to making cards. One thing to remember is to relax and have fun, (color outside the lines) that will show in the ultimate creation of your masterpiece of love.

CARDMAKING TOOLS

- The Ultimate Guide to the Perfect Card-is definitely a must have for an abundance of verses and poems for the perfect sentiments
- Pens-lots of them, different colors, thicknesses, shapes, types, metallic, watercolor, charcoal, etc.
- Templates-there are an abundance available to create all shapes and sizes of cards and notes for every occasion, remember the great software, too
- Keep a pocket size thesaurus and dictionary with all your cardmaking tools. I am always referring to the thesaurus so I don't keep repeating myself. It also helps to get the creative juices flowing and expands your vocabulary at the same time.
- Paper-varying sizes, colors, textures, thicknesses, shapes, and thins; velum and gloss, too, envelopes
- Chalks to use for that extra soft look
- Decorative scissors and punches
- Paper cutter-mini size works for most cutting
- Accordion folder-keeps papers organized
- Notebook to list favorite quotes or jot down ideas and thoughts that come to you.
- Rubberstamps, Die cuts, Eraser, White Out, etc.
- Embellishments of your choosing
- Stickers, glue, ribbon, lace, glitter, jewels, etc.

A Must Have ~
The Ultimate Guide to the Perfect Card

CARDMAKING TIPS

S et up a special place just for you to work on your cardmaking projects. Make the ambiance soft and inviting, too. Try some soft music, a scented candle and some aromatic tea to sip as you allow your imagination to seek the perfect design and wording. Be sure to have a chair that is proper for your body and plenty of table space with good lighting to ensure comfort.

- ◎ Cardmaking is good for the soul, so consider this an enchanting time of being alone with yourself.

- ◎ Find a quiet place to sit and create. Solitude enhances creativity, allowing feelings to flow.

- ◎ If you get stuck on what to write:
    - ~ refer to the tips in my book
    - ~ think about who you are creating for
    - ~ take a break and sip some tea
    - ~ ask yourself what your heart wants to say

- ◎ Think about the person for whom you are creating the card to determine the type of card you want to create. Make a list of all the cards you will be needing to send this year and add some extra.

- ◎ Try to make several cards at once if they are for similar events. You can personalize them for each occasion, but this will give you selection on hand when the need arises. It's also just as easy to create several of the same card at one time.

- ◎ Don't forget to decorate the envelope, too. It adds to the uniqueness of the card.

ThENa's ThougHTS

For those people not fluent enough to write letters and mushy notes, a card is an acceptable means of expressing everything from love to humor. Often we know what feelings we want to express but are at a loss for words. True, there is nothing new under the sun, for down through history men and women have shared these same feelings and since the beginning of the creating and exchanging of cards, these feelings have been expressed. But we're always looking for something different.

Almost everyday I get requests for verses for birthdays, new baby congratulations, a thank you to teacher, friend or pastor. The writer usually prefaces it with "I just cannot write, but…" and then pours out beautiful thoughts from their heart. They have written the verse in their hearts but just need help getting it down on paper.

As you write your card, whether prose or poetry, think about what you want to say, what does the person mean to you and what do you feel in your heart. If you write down even a few key words, you can go back and elaborate on your thoughts.

If I have a request for a special card for a wedding, an engagement, sympathy, or special birthday card, I ask God to give me something that will touch that person's heart and express what they want to say and what the recipient needs to hear. Many times I receive notes back asking me how I knew what their hopes, fears or dreams were and my answer is that I didn't, but God knows and I still think it is amazing that in this vast universe He still will answer my little requests to bless someone with a special verse.

Hugs, Thena

POEMS

Sentiments

QUOTES

AND

Expressions

THE HISTORY OF THE GREETING CARD

The modern custom of sending greeting cards can be traced back through the centuries. The valentine is considered to be the original ancestor of today's greeting cards. The Germans printed New Year's greetings from woodcuts as early as the year 1400.

Esther A. Howland was a pioneer in the American valentine manufacturing industry. In 1847, she became fascinated with the idea of making valentines using scraps of paper, lace and ribbons. With the help of her friends, she was America's first assembly-line producer of high-quality lacy valentines.

Louis Prang, in Boston, is primarily credited with the start of the greeting card industry in America. In the early 1870s, he began the publication of deluxe editions of Christmas cards, which found a ready market in England. In 1875, Prang introduced the first complete line of Christmas cards to the American public.

By the late 1950s, there were hundreds of greeting card publishers who produced about five billion cards, with half of those being Christmas cards. Over seven billion greeting cards for all occasions are purchased annually in the United States.

Handmade cards have come full circle. We are taking our cue from Esther Howland and using our "scraps" to craft personal works of art for our family and friends.

A sincere thanks to "Simply Sentiments" magazine for their generosity in allowing us to share excerpts from this article in their premiere issue debuting January/February 2004. For the complete article, please be sure to visit them online www.simplysentiments.com or contact them through the information in the "Resource" section of this book.

Expressing Yourself

The perfect card should communicate, celebrate and commemorate the occasion for which it was created to the person it was created for.

Communicate: \Com*mu'ni*cate\, v 1. To impart; to bestow; to convey 2. transmit thoughts or feelings

To impart your feelings should be the goal in your card. Letting the recipient know that you are with him in spirit and emotion on whatever occasion this might be is important. So many times we receive generic cards, with generic sentiments and never really know what the sender is feeling. Through this simple card you can express a range of emotions from affection, ardor, concern or desire to elation, grief, passion or sympathy. So making communication of your feelings the main focus in your cardmaking will result in a blessing to the recipient.

Celebrate: \Cel'e*brate\, v. 1. To observe an event or day with ceremonies of respect, festivity, or rejoicing.

The card you create should reflect the mood of the occasion. Is it a solemn, joyous, miraculous, passionate or spiritual time? Whatever the mood, the concept of your card should symbolize the event through color, design, embellishment and sentiment. At a glance, your heartfelt emotions will speak to the heart of the recipient and evoke feelings relative to the occasion, through your design. Everyone wants to feel special, no matter what the tone of an event. We all need to feel like we matter and nothing says that more than the giving of our time. The fact that you would take the time to create something totally unique to the event says so much about your heart.

Celebrate   COMMUNICATE

Commemorate: \Com*mem'o*rate\, v. 1. To call to remembrance by a special act or observance; to celebrate with honor and solemnity; to honor, as a person or event, by some act of respect or affection, intended to preserve the remembrance of the person or event. 2. keep alive the memory of someone

Think of how often we search for the perfect words to say or write, or the perfect gift to buy. For many of us, it is important that a particular event or time be kept close to our hearts. Think about picture taking. We all want pictures that will capture a specific moment. So it is with a card. Let your card capture the moment and be a cherished memory that can be touched and remembered for generations to come. Whatever the occasion, because that moment was a special time in the history of the recipient's life, you will want to express the importance by incorporating all of the above elements in your creations.

Card making allows you to be creative and express yourself with a very personal touch. There are a host of occasions where a handmade card would be a wonderful gesture. From Anniversaries, to Birthdays, to Weddings and more, cards can be created using the simplest of techniques and products or you can get elaborate and create an elegant piece of art. Either way, because you took the time to make it, the recipient will feel very special.

Technique is limited only by your imagination. There are some basics to remember that will add to a more attractive card. I won't elaborate much here, because there are many books, magazines and websites available that will take you to new heights in your cardmaking techniques and keep you apprised of the latest in trendy and traditional products for all your cardmaking needs and wants.

Commemorate

For those of you into scrapbooking and rubber-stamping, you already know the endless supplies available to create the perfect page and thus it's a natural to transfer these same techniques and use the same products for cardmaking. For those who are not familiar with these wonderful crafts, you're in for a treat. Being a newcomer to the scrapping world, there appears to be an endless supply of products that would allow you to create a magnificent masterpiece. Finding these products and learning about techniques is easy, too. It's just like being a kid in a candy store.

For starters, visiting your local scrapbook or rubberstamp stores will introduce you to such an incredible array of products and educational materials to create projects such as cards, note cards, gift tags, gift wrap, bookmarks, certificates, awards, invitations and so much more. Many stores hold classes on a regular basis to help educate, as well as share the experience with fellow crafters.

While you're at the stores, it would benefit you to check out the latest in magazines available that can teach you and treat you to the latest and greatest materials you might want. Listed in the Resource Section of my book is information about a few of the popular magazines available. Be sure to check them out, especially Simply Sentiments, the brand new magazine designed specifically with cardmakers in mind.

Check out the Resource Section

Once you've explored all the stores in your area and still need more materials, be sure to get online and visit all the online stores. I've listed a few in the Resource Section for your convenience, but there are so many that it is impossible for me to list them all. Sometimes you can find things online that aren't available anywhere else and vice versa.

Now that you have all your materials (o.k., a few,) you're probably wondering where to begin. Well, once you've read all you can in the magazines you've acquired, attended every class in nine counties of local rubberstamping and scrapbooking stores, never fear there's more yet!

When I started writing my book and researching this pastime, I was absolutely blown away by the endless amount of information and products available through the Internet for all of you cardmaking, rubberstamping and scrapbooking addicts. If you want to learn technique, there are unlimited people on the web showcasing talents and explaining the techniques used to create their latest new creations.

There are also an abundance of newsletters and magazines available only online. Some are available for free, others for a nominal fee. I believe most are open to accepting submissions from their readers, too, which makes it wonderful for a newcomer to this craft, because the ideas presented are almost unlimited. The talent that is abounding is awe-inspiring, too. Again, I have listed a few in my Resource Section for your convenience.

MATERIALS   technique

Then when you still want more, you will definitely want to check out some of the message boards for tips and techniques from the amateurs and the professionals. Many of the major magazines and some of the big companies have their own boards, as do the smaller online stores. There are also message boards that are just that and nothing more.

To be honest, there are so many resources available for cardmakers, scrappers and stampers to create a card by hand or on their computer, I am learning about them all the time. It's a good thing they weren't all stores in my neighborhood, because I would get lost. Lost, but I'd be having fun shopping, too! The point is that you'll have fun with all the window-shopping you can do.

My first suggestion is create a list of specific cards you want to make throughout the year and begin to create a detailed list of necessary supplies and a wish list, too. Keep them in a small notebook and carry it with you on your shopping sprees, whether it's traveling to a local store or elsewhere or simply your online surfing ventures. You will find that this will save you time and money and help you to avoid purchasing duplicate materials. In a sense it's kind of like buying clothes. While it's all well and good to have a variety of clothes in an array of colors, styles, shapes and sizes, if you don't have some coordination and semblance of organization, it can become a very confusing time selecting an outfit, to say nothing of the potential for being on the worst-dressed list for the year. Seriously, how many times have you gone to your closet with an article of clothing in hand and guess what, there's nothing that matches.

Cards

I have literally given away items after years with the tags still on because of this very thing. I must say that my scrapbook armoire, in my living room, was beginning to look that way until I decided to try to plan ahead. I can tell you this makes for a more peaceful time when I finally get down to creating my projects and saves me money, also.

I hope this tip helps, so when you go shopping you will have a plan. I'm not saying don't buy those sweet little doo-dads that you love and know will look so beautiful on "something." I'm just suggesting if one has a plan, they will be economically better off than if you just shop so impulsively.

Now let's see what are the basics we need to make this a fun and inspiring time...

- ◎ Your little space with a comfortable table or desk and chair
- ◎ Warm and inviting with good lighting all around
- ◎ Soft music to help the creative juices flow
- ◎ Plenty of cardstock for your cards, tags, envelopes
- ◎ Lots of different color papers in a variety of weights and textures
- ◎ Simple tools such as scissors, tape, glue or other adhesives, paper cutters, punches, pens, paints, chalks
- ◎ Embossing items, rubberstamps, inks, etc.

The Basics

- Idea books and your magazine collection
- Embellishments to your heart's content ranging from stickers of all shapes, sizes, textures, styles, glitter, jewels, ribbons, lace, eyelets, rub-ons, and the list goes on.
- A computer, your favorite software and a color printer. There are a variety of programs available, some are graphic programs in general with special templates and then there are others specifically designed for cardmaking.

A must have that will help you in finding
just the right words are my books:

THE ULTIMATE GUIDE TO THE PERFECT WORD &
THE ULTIMATE GUIDE TO THE PERFECT CARD

With supplies
in my hands
I use my love
of my art to create a card
for you straight from
my heart

~ Thena Smith

Let the creating begin ~

ACROSS THE MILES

- Absence extinguishes small passions and increases great ones, as the wind blows out a candle, and fans a bonfire.
- As I look out the window, I see us walking hand in hand... and I know even with the miles now between us, we are still walking heart in heart. – CC Milam
- Coming from far away, to wish you a blessed day!
- Distance makes the heart grow fonder.
- From ocean to ocean and sea to sea, nothing can separate my love for thee. – CC Milam
- Here I am and there you are, but in my heart we are not that far. – CC Milam
- Here is a hug in your mailbox from Me!
- May the Lord keep watch between you and me when we are away from each other. – Genesis 31:49 NIV
- No miles of any measurement can separate your soul from mine. – Antonio Suave
- So far away it brightens my day to remember your smiles across the miles. – Jennifer Byerly
- There is one pain I often feel, which you'll never know. It's caused by the absence of you. – Ashleigh
- Time has brought us to this place where you are there and I am here. – CC Milam

Somewhere between your heart and mine
Is a long distance of time and space...
I miss you through all the miles and
Dream of the day I will again see your face.
– CC Milam

Distance between two hearts is not an
obstacle...rather a beautiful reminder
of just how strong true love can be.

When we are apart from each other,
I will remember when I met you,
Your eyes told me to fall in love with you
And I followed your heart to a place where
I could be happy and I will stay there
For the rest of my life... I Love You

Dear Brother

I wish I could see you more often
But know that for what it is worth
My love is always beside you
No matter where you are on earth
For the bond that I feel with you brother
Is one that no distance can break
And I so often think of you fondly
At night while I'm lying awake
I smile at the memories and moments
As siblings that we'll always share
I'm so proud that you are my brother
And I carry that pride everywhere
So I'm hoping throughout as you're reading
This message and then when you're done
You'll know just how much I love you
And admire the man you've become!
– Jennifer Byerly

A card in my mailbox keeps the
blues at bay when you travel far...
and away from me stay...
Missing You
~ CC Milam

ANGELS

- A kind soul is inspired by angels.
- An angel can fly directly into the heart of the matter.
- An angel in the house they say, will guard your family night and day.
- Angel smiles are the next best thing to halos.
- Angels–Don't leave home without 'em.
- Angels are never too distant to hear you.
- Angels carry messages of love.
- Angels may not come when you call them, but they'll always be there when you need them.
- Angels from up above, please protect the ones we love.
- Angels welcome here
- Be an Angel–Practice random acts of kindness.
- Be not forgetful to entertain strangers: for thereby some have entertained angels unawares. – Hebrews 13:2 KJV
- Every blade of grass has its angel that bends over it and whispers, "Grow, Grow." – The Talmud
- Friends are angels on earth.
- Guardian Angels touch our lives through friendships.
- Guardian Angels work on a wing and a prayer.
- Happy is the heart that believes in angels.
- Like snowflakes, no two angels are alike.
- Miracles happen to those who believe in angels.
- My guardian angel has a tough job.
- The angel of the Lord encamps around those who fear Him, and rescues them. – Psalm 34:7 NIV
- When a child is born, the angels sing.
- Wherever you go, whatever you do, may the angels watch over you.

All night, all day,
Angels watching over me, my Lord
All night, all day,
Angels watching over me.

Sun is a-setting in the West;
Angels watching over me, my Lord.
Sleep my child, take your rest;
Angels watching over me.

All night, all day,
Angels watching over me, my Lord.
All night, all day,
Angels watching over me.

I gazed upon an angel
Sleeping soundly in her bed
And as I watched her breathing
Visions filled my head...
~ Barbara Cox

I know there are girl angels
I see one every day.
She gives me a hug
And kisses my cheek,
And then runs to play.
From her toothless smile
She's my little angel
Sweet as you please.

For He will command His angels concerning
you to guard you in all your ways.
~ Psalm 91:11 NIV

ANNiVeRSaRy

- ◎ Always
- ◎ Anniversary wishes and kisses
- ◎ Before us lies eternity where our souls shall never part.
- ◎ Best Wishes on your happy occasion
- ◎ Celebrate your love together
- ◎ Congratulations, job well done!
- ◎ Dancing through the years together
- ◎ Each day is an Anniversary with you
- ◎ Endless Love Stories
- ◎ Even now–crazy after all these years
- ◎ Everlasting–a love that is true
- ◎ Memories with you are endless as the stars
- ◎ Fairy tales do last forever
- ◎ Forever in Love
- ◎ Happy Anniversary–You did it!
- ◎ I got you babe
- ◎ I have found the one whom my soul loves. – Song of Solomon
- ◎ I love being married to my best friend!
- ◎ I may grow old, but my heart will never grow tired of loving you.
- ◎ I still only have eyes for you.
- ◎ I'd say "I do" all over again...
- ◎ In a marriage where love abides–is a home shared side by side.
- ◎ In honor of your love together
- ◎ In time, love comes full circle and is revealed in simple memories built by trust. – LaTourelle
- ◎ Love is a circle without end, willing to give and ready to bend. – LaTourelle

- Love is a journey that began at forever & ends at never.
- Love reasons the heart and confounds the mind. – LaTourelle
- Me and You & You and Me
- Remember the Romance
- Still living happily ever after
- Still looking like newlyweds–young and in love
- The Fairy Tale Continues
- The love you share all these years makes this day special for all who know and love you.
- To a beautiful couple
- To Thee with All My Heart
- True love stories never have endings
- Two hearts still beating as one
- When a man loves a woman
- When two souls meet…Love begins
- You and Me against the world
- You're a beautiful couple

*Through the years it's better everyday,
through the years God always made a way,
through the years together we shall stay.*

Love suffereth long, and is kind; Love envieth not; Love vaunteth not itself, is not puffed up. Doth not behave itself unseemly, seeketh not her own, is not easily provoked, thinketh no evil; rejoiceth not in iniquity, but rejoiceth in the truth; beareth all things, believeth all things, hopeth all things, endureth all things. Love never faileth... – 1 Corinthians 13:4-8 KJV

What greater thing is there for two human souls than to feel that they are joined together to strengthen each other in all labor, to minister to each other in all sorrows, to share with each other in all gladness, to be one with each other in the silent unspoken memories?
— George Elliot

So Jacob served seven years to get Rachel, but they seemed like only a few to him because of his love for her
— Book of Genesis

Marriage is popular because it combines the maximum of temptation with the maximum of opportunity. Happy Anniversary
— George Bernard Shaw

You were made perfectly to be loved and surely I have loved you, the idea of you, my whole life long.
— Elizabeth Barrett Browning

My darling love, they say the best is yet to be
So with thy heart, come grow old with me
Memories we shall build with blessings to treasure
Side by side, with a love that has no measure
— LaTourelle

She is a winsome wee thing,
She is a handsome wee thing,
She is a lo'esome wee thing,
This sweet wee wife o' mine.
~ Robert Burns

*Many waters cannot quench love,
neither can floods drown it.*
~ Song of Solomon

My love for you through the years
Has grown so steadily
Proving to my heart and soul
That a couple we were meant to be.
– Thena Smith

*The secret to your happy marriage
must be those two little words...*
"Yes, Dear!"

Thank you for the joys and sorrows
Looking forward to all our tomorrows

*Slow dancing together after
all these years and loving it...*

For You on Our Anniversary My Love~
The minute I heard my first love story
I started looking for you,
Not knowing how blind that was.
Lovers don't finally meet somewhere.
They're in each other all along.
– Rumi

FiRST YEAR

- After one year you're still my one and only!
- Blended as One
- Happy 1st Anniversary
- Happy Anniversary and more to come
- Happy Anniversary to a One-derful couple!
- It's been a year???
- I promised "I do" forever.
- Love is the beginning—Love is the end
- Number one, the fun's just begun!
- One isn't lonely when it's one year with you!
- One year and still going strong
- One year and still saying, "I do"
- One year of joy, one year of fun, the best part of marriage has only begun. - Jennifer Byerly
- One year together and a zillion more
- One year with my best friend
- One year with you and heading for two!
- One year! It's a count up to love!
- One year... You made it!
- Our love is like the Energizer Bunny... everlasting!
- Our marriage belongs in the Land of Awwwwwws...
- Stay tuned for next year's episodes...
- The Honeymoon Continues
- Two hearts, one love, one year
- You and me against the world.
- Thinking of our 1st year together... You are such a gift... I want to "wrap" my arms around you. - Jennifer Byerly
- You've only just begun

Of all the joys in a long and happy life,
There's none so precious as the love
Between husband and wife.
May your years ahead be blessed
With a wonderful journey.

One year together and
Still one hundred years
Will still be too few to
Be in love with you.
– LaTourelle

You wear your love and joyfulness
As a husband and a wife
By looking like the last year
Is the best year of your life.
So Happy Anniversary
Here's my wish for you:
May the love you had the first year
Double up in number two!
– Jennifer Byerly

One year of marriage together
Oh, how the time has flown
Days of joyous memories
Sometimes nights filled with storm
Through it all your love has grown
Giving you love to continue on...

Love is two hearts beating as one...
It's your 1st year with more to come.

25 Years—Sterling Silver

- After twenty five years of marriage with you I still wake up and wonder if I'm dreaming. - Jennifer Byerly
- First silver then gold, let's grow old–together! - Jennifer Byerly
- Goodness gracious sakes alive! Is it really 25?? - Jennifer Byerly
- Happy 25th to a couple that shines
- How far away the stars seem, how long ago was our first kiss.
- If ever there was love... It began and ended in you.
- I've had twenty five years of my favorite time of year... Our Anniversary! - Jennifer Byerly
- Let's break the bank on love and go for twenty five more!
- Love has kept you together–Love carries you through.
- Silver may be a precious metal... but not as precious as our love! - Jennifer Byerly
- So many years together, you are still sterling as ever. May you shine on through.
- Still ringing like two silver bells
- There's no one else's breath I'd rather wake up next to!
- Through the years your love has endured
- To a precious couple... Still shining with a special love.
- Twenty-five years and still shining like the stars
- Twenty-five years of love–sent from God above
- WOW! 25 years of wedded bliss–May your day be as special as you.

A moment of love wrapped in
Twenty Five years, memories to treasure,
Stories to share... an everlasting love
~ LaTourelle

On Our Silver Anniversary

Though Our Anniversary is silver
Our love is really gold!
Just like the potted treasure
At the rainbow's end we're told!
That's why this day is extra
Special don't you see
Our marriage is a treasure
And it was meant to be!!!
– Jennifer Byerly

Do you love me? Do you love me? After 25 years Why do you ask me now?

~ Fiddler on the Roof

To a Special Couple

An anniversary is a celebration of life and love
and the special memories two people share...
It's a celebration of dreams come true
and reflection of years together and,
most of all, the special love you share.
Happy 25th Anniversary

Through the Years

You are my first thought in the morning,
My strength throughout the day,
The words I whisper sweetly
Every evening when I pray.

50 Years of Golden Grace

- Baby, it's been a sentimental journey with you all the way!
- Fifty years of marriage? It felt like yesterday!
- Golden years filled with sunshine and rain
- In spite of all the hard years, You are still golden to me.
- Only 50 years? And they said it wouldn't last.
- Time has honored the essence of your love in every way.
- We celebrate your love today with praise to God who made the way.
- Year after year you are more precious than gold
- Your love's seen you through again and again...

Fifty years together is a wonderful place to be.
You are a lovely couple sharing many memories.
We celebrate with you on this golden day,
And we give our blessing to you in every way.
– GG Milam

Blessed with a marriage so laden with love. Strengthened and nurtured by God above. Memories and miracles built day by day. Touching many lives in a wonderful way. Today may this love come back to you. For all that you give and all that you do. Happy 50th Anniversary
– LaTourelle

Happy days shared fill the treasure
chest of life with very precious
jewels called memories

On this Our Golden Wedding Day

I pledge my love anew
Look at what our love doth say
We stood the ground and fought the fight
With love that was tested both day and night
Fifty years we have shared together
My darling know this, My Love is Forever
– LaTourelle

Golden like the sun, aged like vintage wine
What a race you've run, built with love divine.
Memories yet untold, blessings to behold
Precious and so rare, this life that you share.
Happy 50th Anniversary
– LaTourelle

Happy olden days
Happy golden days
Fifty years so bright
Shine on forevermore

~ LaTourelle

Golden years so filled with love
Sent to you from God above
Built with blessings and joy so rare
Oh what a treasure you two share!
Many Blessings
– LaTourelle

Still golden after all these years

As life grows older and so do we
May I have this dance with thee
Let us remember the night of glory
When once began our true love story
In my arms, as you waltz to music slow
Share in the memories of long ago
Years so full of joy and sorrow
Every day was a new tomorrow
Still here you are close by my side
Giving in faith, your love doth abide.
– Linda LaTourelle

When you are old and grey and full of sleep,
And nodding by the fire, take down this
book, and slowly read, and dream of the
Soft look your eyes had once, and of their shadows deep;
How many loved your moments of glad grace,
And loved your beauty with love false or true,
But one man loved the pilgrim Soul in you,
And loved the sorrows of your changing face;
And bending down beside the glowing bars,
Murmur, a little sadly, how Love fled
And paced upon the mountains overhead
And hid his face amid a crowd of stars.   – Yeats

Did you never know, long ago, how much you
loved me, that your love would never lessen
and never go? You were young then, proud
and fresh-hearted, you were too young to know.
– Sara Teasdale

If ever two were one, then surely we.
If ever man were loved by wife, then thee.
If ever wife was happy in a man,
Compare with me, ye woman, if you can.
I prize thy love more than whole mines of gold,
Or all the riches that the East doth hold.
My love is such that rivers cannot quench,
Nor ought but love from thee, give recompense.
Thy love is such I can no way repay:
The heavens reward thee manifold, I pray.
The while we live, in love let's so persevere,
That when we live no more, we may live ever.
– Anne Bradstreet

Fifty years have come and passed
And so quickly the time has gone
Those who think that love fades with time
Are very very wrong.

My love for you through the years
Has grown so steadily
Proving to my heart and soul
That a couple we were meant to be.
– Thena Smith

Through the years,
the good times and the bad,
you've given all you had and
Love has brought you to this day.

Happy 50th

A man, a wife
Began their life
Many years ago

They pledged their love
Before God above
With vows that made it so

All could see
'Twas meant to be
And there would be no other

Two hearts as one
When the day was done
Made for one another
– Jennifer Byerly

Fifty years together
And they said it'd never last
Still walking side by side
Sharing memories of the past
Happy Golden Years
– LaTourelle

What a golden celebration
We are wishing you today
With love and joy
To share in everyway
Always and Forever

APOLOGY

- An apology is a good way to have the last word.
- Can I buy your forgiveness??? Visa or MasterCard??
- Did I say I was–WRONG? I was!
- Forgive me, please...
- Forgiven?
- Guilty, Guilty, Guilty
- Here are some pretty flowers. I picked them myself...
- How can I say I'm sorry? I only speak one language.
- How do you spell forgiveness?
- I'm not really sure what really happened but all I can do is ask for you to forgive me.
- I'm sincerely sorry
- I owe you this "I'm sorry" card
- I was mistaken
- I was wrong!
- I wish I'd learn to keep my foot in my mouth!
- If your brother sins, rebuke him, and if he repents, forgive him. – Luke 17:3 NIV
- I'll be sorry if you will be sorry
- My behavior and my manners are really sorry.
- O.K. I blew it!
- O.K. I'm sorry–but it really was your fault!
- Please forgive me, I know not what I do.
- Same old story, same old song, please forgive me.
- Sorry, I didn't mean it or I guess that I was wrong
- Whoever I was, says, "Sorry."
- Yep, it was MY fault–SORRY!
- Yes, I'll sleep in the doghouse but just for tonight...

I'm praying that you will forgive me for my actions
and my words. I did not mean to hurt your feelings.
Will you please forgive me?

Do you still love me? Let's kiss and
makeup together and move forward.

If you fill your heart with regrets of
Yesterday and the worries of tomorrow,
You have no today to be thankful for.
I'm ready to move forward
And leave the past in the past.

Bear with each other and forgive whatever grievances
you may have against one another. Forgive as the
Lord forgave you. - Colossians 3:13 NIV

Sorry can be an awful word
If one does not know they are forgiven
But when accepted in a loving way
It brings one closer to Heaven.
~ Thena Smith

Saying I'm sorry is not an easy thing to do.
I really did not mean to show mistrust in you.
Sorry for the way my words came out.
All I can do is ask for your forgiveness
And hope deep in your heart that you can
forgive me and us still be friends
- GG Milam

Never apologize for showing feeling. When you do so, you apologize for truth.   – Benjamin Disraeli

An apology is the superglue of life. It can repair just about anything.   – Lynn Johnston

Forgiveness is the fragrance the violet sheds on the heel that has crushed it.   – Mark Twain

The weak can never forgive. Forgiveness is the attribute of the strong.   – Mahatma Gandhi

'Tis better to argue a point and not settle it, than to settle a point and not argue it. – J. Joubert

Apology is a lovely perfume; it can transform the clumsiest moment into a gracious gift. – Margaret Runbeck

Forgiveness is a funny thing. It warms the heart and cools the sting.   – William Arthur Ward

Always forgive your enemies–nothing annoys them as much.   – Oscar Wilde

And when you stand praying, if you hold anything against anyone, forgive him, so that your Father in heaven may forgive you your sins. But if you do not forgive, neither will your Father who is in heaven forgive your sins.   – Mark 11:25 NIV

BABY SHOWER

- A baby is an inestimable blessing and a bother. – Mark Twain
- A gift from God above
- A miracle is on the way
- Baby ~ Just another WORD for Love!
- Babies are blessings sent from above.
- Baby's have a way of changing our hearts and lives forever.
- Baby's breath so soft and sweet with tiny hands and feet.
- Come and celebrate the birth of the cutest kid on earth!
- Congratulations on your gift from heaven!
- For the proud parents-to-be
- For you and the baby on the way
- God bless you on your new adventure as parents.
- Little feet, oh, how sweet!
- Nothing like a new baby to bring us joy, whether it is a girl or boy! – Thena Smith
- Nothing smells sweeter than a baby
- Our hearts rejoice with you
- Pink and Blue and a present for you
- Sharing in your joy
- Shower the Mommy-to-be
- The greatest gift
- There's a new world of wonder for you & your new baby.
- Tiny little baby boy filling our happy home with joy!
- Tiny little baby girl bringing joy to our world!
- What a celebration of life!
- What an exciting day and hour. Time to celebrate with a shower! – Thena Smith
- Wishes on a new beginning
- You and me and baby makes three

A precious little baby
we celebrate today,
With good wishes I have
brought to send her/his way.
– Sharon Ezzell

Bring a little something
To share in the special day
Of _____ and _____
And the baby soon to come
A special little blessing
In the form of daughter or son!
– Thena Smith

Little ones need parents
Who are warm and loving, too,
Parents who put kindness
into everything they do…
Parents who put laughter,
And happy noise and fun–
That's why you'll be perfect parents
For your precious little one!

Tiny fingers and tiny toes
All lined up in little rows.
~ CC Milam

This quilt is just for baby
It's made with loving care
Each stitch comes with a special
Heartfelt grandma prayer
In hopes that baby grows up
One day to understand
She was also crafted
By the maker's hand!
– Jennifer Byerly

Fresh fallen from the heavens
A baby from above
A precious little gem
Sent for you to love
   – Jennifer Byerly

Not of your flesh, but still she
Is yours forever more
To care for and to cherish
Nourish and adore!
   – Jennifer Byerly

A precious baby girl (boy)
Sent from God above
Delivered by an angel
On the wings of love
   – Jennifer Byerly

Showers of blessings
A baby to love
What a gift from heaven
Sent with God's love.
   – LaTourelle

Dearest Little Child
Precious in our sight
What a joyous blessing
You brought us tonight.
   – LaTourelle

*The Lord has blessed you from
above with a precious baby to love*

A Baby is...

Smiles and laughter and coos
Wonder and softness and sweet lullabies,
Beauty that shines like the starlight above,
But first, last and foremost... a baby is love.

Soft chubby cheeks and a diaper that leaks
Always at play-through the night and the day-
Cuddles so sweet and smelly little feet
Hands on the go and always hears "no"
And so is life with a baby to love...
– GG Milam

Soon your little one will arrive and have
you to call "Mommy" and "Daddy."
Until then, wait patiently and treasure
your few moments alone as a couple!
May you find joy in the days ahead as
you plan for your new family.

Loving a baby is a circular business, a kind of feedback loop. The more you give the more you get and the more you get the more you feel like giving. – Penelope Leach

Making the decision to have a child-it's momentous. It is to decide forever to have your heart go walking around outside your body.
– Elizabeth Stone

A baby is a full time job for three adults. Nobody tells you that when you're pregnant, or you'd probably jump off a bridge. Nobody tells you how all-consuming it is to be a mother and how reading goes out the window and thinking too.
– Erica Jong

BaPTiSM

In my heart I have such joy
Over-seeing the choice you made today
Such joy that could not be expressed
By any words that I might say

But I've stored in a very place
The awesome memories of this day
And be assured that for the rest of my life
They will be treasured and replayed
– Thena Smith

Baptism is the gift of God's Love
The celebration of a precious
New child in His world.

Oh, what a wonderful blessed day
I know God hears every prayer I pray
For here you are honoring the Father and Son
By being baptized, my little one!
– Thena Smith

We watched your face
As we held you
And the minister baptized you
In the Name of the Father,
The Son and Holy Spirit,
And we felt such a thrill
Knowing that we were introducing
You, young as you are
To doing the Father's will.
– Thena Smith

On Your Dedication to the Lord

Today we come together to
Present you before the Lord.
To give you back to Him
To love and adore.
Blessings
– GG Milam

With joy in my heart
I celebrate this day with you
And always will be here for you
Wherever you are and whatever you do
~ Thena Smith

Lord, look down from heaven above
Touch this child with your wonderful love
Guide and protect this little one
Throughout each hour until day is done
On your dedication to the Lord
Today we come together
To present you before the Lord
To give you back to Him
To love and adore
– Thena Smith

Blessings to you on the Special Day
As you are brought before the Lord

On Your Dedication

God places children in our lives
To care for and to love
That's why we dedicate them
To our Father up above
We pray they'll always hunger for
His living word each day
Learning by example
And through the words we say
Because the Lord entrusted us
We'll do our very best
To teach them each to follow Him
So they may too be blessed!
— Jennifer Byerly

God loves you and cherishes you
For you are a treasure
His love for you exceeds
Anything that can be measured
And this day is an answered prayer
That this moment in your life I could share.
May God bless you on this special day
And send peace, love and joy your way.
— Thena Smith

May joy and happiness fill your heart
As this new day has set you apart
With honor to our God above
May you feel His presence and His love.
— Thena Smith

We come today to dedicate this child
Unto the Lord. To our precious child,
May the Lord bless you today & always

Bar Mitzvah

- May your Bar Mitzvah day bring you a sense of pride and accomplishment.
- Mazel Tov on your Bar Mitzvah
- She is a tree of life to those who embrace her; those who lay hold of her will be blessed. - Proverbs 3:18 NIV
- This is a very special time for you and your family, today and throughout a future of bright promises.
- Wishing you a hearty Mazel Tov on your special day when you are called up to read from the Torah!
- With faith, there are no questions; without faith there are no answers. - The Chofetz Chaim
- You have studied and all the hard work has paid off!

Celebrate your Bar Mitzvah
May this special day
Fill you with faith that will
Strengthen you and inspire you.

In seeking wisdom
The first step in silence,
The second: listening,
The third: remembering,
The fourth: practicing,
The fifth: teaching others.
- Gabirol

May your hearts be
blessed with faith
that grows and joy
that lasts forever.

BiRTh

- A Blessing from Heaven
- A Star is Born
- Baby You're a Rich Man
- Boy Meets World
- Celebrating New Life
- Child is Born
- God gave me His Love—God gave me you!
- His Name is Wonderful
- In the Beginning
- Life Has Begun
- Miracle Baby
- Miracles Do Happen
- More Than Wonderful
- Now Appearing
- Our Dream Come True
- Our Family has grown by two feet
- Our Family is Complete
- Our New Little Star
- Sweet Beginnings
- The Greatest Thing
- The Miracle of Life
- There's a Kind Of Hush
- This Just In
- Tiny hands and Tiny feet
- We have entered a "changing" world
- Welcome Little One
- Welcome to the World, Little One
- We've Only Just Begun

A tiny little baby
So innocent and sweet
Will bring love and happiness
And make your family complete

What are little boys made of?
What are little boys made of?
Frogs and snails,
And puppy-dogs' tails;
That's what little boys are made of.

What are little girls made of?
What are little girls made of?
Sugar and spice,
and all that's nice;
That's what little girls are made of.

Of your flesh I may not be a part
Our love was born from God's very heart.
~ Thena Smith

Thinking of you on this special day
That the Lord would bless you in everyway

What a beautiful blessing from the Lord!
Rejoicing with you in the birth
of your precious little one
~ CC Milam

We just never dreamed that she'd be so wonderful
We feel so very thankful for her precious little soul!
- Jennifer Byerly

For you created my inmost being;
you knit me together in my mother's womb.
I praise you because I am fearfully and wonderfully made;
your works are wonderful,
I know that full well.
My frame was not hidden from you
when I was made in the secret place.
When I was woven together in the depths of the earth,
your eyes saw my unformed body.
All the days ordained for me
were written in your book
before one of them came to be.
– Psalm 139: 13-16 NIV

What blessing surpasses all others
Then the tug on a grandma's heart strings?
As she cradles the next generation
And the joy that her grandbaby brings!
Light of her life and so precious!
Oh how she makes her heart sing!
Sweet goodness fresh fallen from heaven
Delivered on soft angel wings
– Jennifer Byerly

Pink or blue with ten little toes
Soft rosie cheeks and a cute little nose
A gift from the Lord sent from above
Given to you to cherish and love.
Congratulations
– GG Milam

You are so sweet and tiny and new
Everything is so perfect about you
~ Thena Smith

God creates a special gift
In His Heaven above
A gift that is full of joy and laughter

Full of sunshine and of Love
He places all of these wonderful things
Along with a tender heart
Inside a tiny baby girl
And blesses each precious part

He gives her tiny rosebud lips
And the softest baby skin

And just when she seems perfect
He touches her once again
Then he sends her to her family
Through her earthly mom to be
And she blesses all who love her
For all eternity!
I know the Father does these things
That only He could do
For there is no other way to explain
A blessing such as you!
– Thena Smith

God Bless this Child

Tiny little booties
So precious and so sweet
How wonderfully soft are they
On my little one's feet...

Human hands made tiny little socks
For the little one I love
But the precious one who wears them
Was made by God above.

Oh God, I love Thy handiwork!
I'm in awe of all I see,
Especially such a dainty masterpiece
As the child in front of me!
– Thena Smith

God has a way of bringing together
All things that are meant to be
And the joining of baby and parents
Is a glorious sight to see
– Thena Smith

Darling little baby
Bouncing angel boy
Sent to us from God above
To fill our lives with joy!
– Jennifer Byerly

New Baby
I have a new baby brother.
He's as cute as he can be.
And I think he is so lucky
to have a big brother like me!
– Linda Zimmerman

You are the answer to my prayer
You are my dream come true
I asked the Father for a miracle
And He sent me you!
– Thena Smith

Blue booties and a little basketball cap
Toy ponies and a big teddy bear
Are some of the things here and there.
Daddy is a waitin' and Mommy too,
For the big day–the arrival of you!!
– GG Milam

A wee bit of Heaven drifted down from above,
A handful of happiness, a heart full of love,
A blessing was sent your way
Forever in your hearts she will stay.
Blessings on the birth of your daughter

Congratulations!
A Brand new Baby Boy,
To fill your Lives and Hearts with Joy

Getting down on all fours and imitating a rhinoceros stops babies from crying. (Put an empty cigarette pack on your nose for a horn and make loud "snort" noises.) I don't know why parents don't do this more often. Usually it makes the kid laugh. Sometimes it sends him into shock. Either way it quiets him down. If you're a parent, acting like a rhino has another advantage. Keep it up until the kid is a teenager and he definitely won't have his friends hanging around your house all the time.
– P. J. O'Rourke

BIRThDay BLESSINGS

The Land of Birthdays was simply beautiful. To begin with, there was always birthday weather there-brilliant sunshine, blue sky, and a nice little breeze. The trees were always green, and there were always daisies and buttercups growing in the fields.

— Enid Blyton

Birthdays
What a wonderful time to say
You are so special

A Special Prayer for you that God
will bless you on your Birthday

I thank my God every time I remember you.
— Philippians 1:3 NIV

May the Lord bless you on your special day,
today and in everyway.

This is the day the Lord has made;
let us rejoice and be glad in it.
— Psalm 118:24 NIV

Happy Birthday to you,
Happy Birthday to you,
Happy Birthday God Bless You,
Happy Birthday to Yooooouuuu!

Aunt

To a Special Lady in My Life

Thank you Aunt Hazel for being
the best aunt I have ever had.
I love our special friendship and
all the time we spend together.
Thank you for everything you have
taught me about life and myself.
Thank you for all you have given
to me from your heart.
May the Lord Bless You
Happy Birthday
- GG Milam

Wishing you a wonderful birthday
to my most special aunt
Thank you for touching so many with your
simple acts of kindness and love

To My Special Aunt

I love you so much
Birthday Wishes sent with Hugs and Kisses
Happy Birthday with Love

I don't know what I did to deserve a special aunt like you
Someone who always loves me no matter what I do.
So today I'm taking the time to say thank you.
Blessings on your Special Day

Dear Aunt Jane,
You are so sweet, smart, talented,
lovable and just the best!
Are you sure I'm not your child?

Belated Birthday

- ◉ Happy Birthday from a little bit behind-me!
- ◉ Heard you had a great birthday–just heard it a little late! Hope it was great fun–like you!
- ◉ I didn't forget your birthday–I just wanted to help extend the celebration!
- ◉ I didn't forget... I was delayed.
- ◉ I thought about you all day long. Does that count?
- ◉ I'm sorry I missed your birthday–I misplaced my mind somewhere! Belated blessings!
- ◉ I'm not late... I'm early in another time zone.
- ◉ It came. It went. Oops, the card was never sent...
- ◉ Late is such an ugly word. Let's just say this card is promptness challenged!
- ◉ My motto is put off today what you can do tomorrow. I did!!! Happy Birthday, hope it was great!
- ◉ Of course I remembered it was your birthday... I just forgot the date.
- ◉ Oh, I sent you this card late on purpose! I was just prolonging your birthday!
- ◉ Oh, my goodness, me oh, my! I let your birthday slip right on by!
- ◉ Oops–I missed it! Hope it was a day to remember! Just like you! Happy Birthday
- ◉ Out of nowhere came this dog and ate your card...
- ◉ Sorry for missing your important day.
- ◉ Sure it's late, but that's just to catch you off guard! Happy Belated Birthday!
- ◉ You had what? A Birthday? Well, golly–I plum fergot!
- ◉ You look just too young to have had another birthday! And I look so bad to have missed it!

Sorry that my wish is late
But please don't worry
Love and prayers and wishes
Are not to be in a hurry!
– Thena Smith

Sorry I missed your special day
Sorry is really all I can say
Happy Birthday

So today is not your birthday?
I thought for sure that it was...
I'll have to check my calendar and talk
with my personal secretary about that!!
Whenever I hire her!
Hope you had a great day!
– GG Milam

Roses are red and you're a little blue
Oops! Happy Belated Birthday to you!!

What can I say? I'm late. Mom was upset too!
I was late arriving, 9 months and two weeks!!!
Hope you can forgive me.
Oh and by the way... Happy Birthday

Sorry this birthday greeting is a little late
It seems I got a little messed up on the date!

Well, you are always saying that I am always late.
I just did not want to ruin my reputation with you!
I hope you had a great day without my blessing!

Even though your birthday is over
And the night has come
May the first day at your new age
Be happy from the first rising of the sun!

May God send blessings upon blessing
Today and the whole year through
And may His blessings show
Just how special He holds you!
– Thena Smith

I could say I'm a whole lotta early
Or admit I'm a little bit late
Whatever I am I'm sure sorry
This year that you had to wait.

Forget you? Not ever! Don't think so!
I'd be willing to bet my last dime
That the problem I suspicion I'm having
Is the loss of what's left of my mind!

So while it's intact at this moment
I'm sending this message to you
Happy Belated Birthday
For this year and next year too!
– Jennifer Byerly

If I could sing a song for you
I'd sing it loud and clear
I'd sing about your special day
The fact is you're older another year!
But it seems the day is gone and past
May next year not go by so fast!
Hope your day was special in every way.
I'll try to sing next year on your birthday!
– Thena Smith

Brother

- A brother is a friend forever.
- A brother is a little bit of childhood that can never be lost. Thanks for the memories.
- Brothers are a special gift
- Brothers since the beginning Friends 'til the end.
- I know we did not always get along growing up but I'm grateful that we are great friends now.
- I love you like no other. You're a great friend and an incredible brother. - GG Milam
- I'm smiling because you're my brother and I'm laughing cuz there's nothing you can do about it!
- I'm so thankful I have you to call brother.
- It was nice growing up with someone like you- someone to lean on, someone to count on, someone to tell on!
- Oh Brother!
- The best childhood memories I know, I shared with you.
- The best thing about having a brother-I always had a friend to share everything with-except my favorite toy!
- We share childhood memories and grown-up dreams.
- We were-and still are-double trouble.
- What are brothers for if not to share troubles and joys?
- You and me-buddies forever.
- You are my family-you are my brother-through thick and thin until the very end.
- You taught me everything I ever really need to know.

Dear Brother,

Growing up in the house with you really
makes me appreciate my own home!
- GG Milam

Happy Birthday brother
This message comes your way
With smiles and good wishes
Upon your special day!
Since you are turning fifty
Half a century has now passed
May all the years in front of you
Pass by you half as fast
- Jennifer Byerly

Sisters & brothers share special times
Growing up together through the years.
Thinking back over my memories,
I realize that some of my favorite
times are those that we shared.
We could always act crazy and get away with it!
You will always have a special place in my heart
I love you and Happy Birthday
My Brother and My Friend.

I'm so glad God gave me a brother like you!
Thank you for always being there for me through the good
times and the bad. I always knew I had you to come home
to on my bad days to talk it over and on my good days to
share my joy. You are the greatest! Happy Birthday
- GG Milam

Happiness is a brother
So wise and so strong
To guide and protect me
All my life long

Handsome and genuine
A character so true
How blessed is a sister
To have a brother like you
- Shanda Purcell

Children

- Born to Party
- Fantastic Fours
- Finally 6 and full of tricks
- Forever Young
- Happy Birthday to You
- Happy Day
- Have a Dino-mite birthday
- Hey, I'm One and a whole year is done
- I Just turned 6
- A teenager now!
- I'm Finally 7
- It's Great–I'm 8
- It's party time!
- Just One and on the run!
- Let me eat cake
- Look at me–I'm 3
- Look I'm 7–going on 11
- Look who's 2–much to do
- Make a wish
- Now I am (age), I'm clever as clever can be
- Now I'm 5–I can jive!
- Now I'm 9 and the world is mine.
- Now Look Who's 4
- Now See Who's ___ !
- Parties are wonderful!
- Princess for the Day
- Ready, Set, Blow
- Silly Sixes
- Simply Seven
- So I think that I'll be (age) now for ever and ever
- So many presents, so little time!
- Special Memories
- The Party's Here
- There's no time like the presents
- To My Little Wonder
- Wow, Now I'm ___
- Your birthday is a celebration of you
- Your eyes shine and sparkle–just like you!

- It's your Birthday
  So let's celebrate!
  With ice cream, gifts,
  And birthday cake!

- Today is the day that
  we come to you and say
  We love you bunches &
  Happy Birthday

- Roses may be red
  Violets may be blue
  Sugar may be sweet
  But none as sweet as you.

I'm cooking up a party
Please join me for some fun
Won't you stir my laughter up
By saying you will come!
– Jennifer Byerly

Hooray what fun
We just can't wait
Please come help us celebrate!
We'll play games
And so much more
Someone special's turning four!
– Jennifer Byerly

2nd Birthday

Birthday wishes and butterfly kisses
Someone's turning two!
When the day is done we'll have had some fun
With the running and playing we'll do
We'll flutter about and laugh and shout
And giggle the day away
So bring your grin and please join in
As we celebrate her day!
– Jennifer Byerly

4th Birthday

Please join us as we celebrate
Open presents, eat some cake
Someone special's turning four
We'll have fun and so much more!
– Jennifer Byerly

What has been happening?
Where have I been?
How did it happen
That you are turning ten!
– Thena Smith

A yummy birthday cake
Some presents just for you
____ spankings for each year
And perhaps a pinch or two!
- Jennifer Byerly

I wish you lots of laughter
And lots of hugs & kisses
May your dreams come true
Including birthday wishes!
- Jennifer Byerly

I don't know how you grew up
Without me seeing it going on
But suddenly there are candles
A cake, and the birthday song!!
- Thena Smith

Happy Birthday little one
We are so glad today
To bring out the cake and candles
To celebrate your birthday!
- Thena Smith

To a little princess on her birthday,
May all your dreams come true,
May your day be filled with wonder
Is the wish I have for you.
- Sharon Ezzell

Someone's having a birthday
So look into this mirror
That's her looking back at you
What a birthday dear!
- Jennifer Byerly

Another year of loving you
Another year of joy
Another year to add to my
Darling birthday boy!
– Jennifer Byerly

Happy Birthday little one
We are so glad today
To bring out the cake and candles
To celebrate your birthday!
– Thena Smith

It's a day to celebrate
It's a day above all the rest
Happy (age) Birthday
We hope it's the best!
– GG Milam

It's your birthday
And we think you're neat
That's why we are sending
This little birthday treat!
– Thena Smith

Howdy, birthday boy
May today you have some fun
And may your day be a happy one!
– GG Milam

Itsy bitsy spider Rock n' roll or rap
There will always be a place for you
On your mother's lap!
– Jennifer Byerly

Happy birthday to you in all
Different shapes and sizes
In each box may
You get lots of surprises!
– GG Milam

Wishing you sunshine, love, and laughter
Not just today but all the days after.
Happy Birthday

I tried and tried to make you a gift
And found it really hard.
So I hope you like your present,
It's this pretty card!
– GG Milam

Your birthday is a day to remember
And finds me thinking too
That the world is much nicer
Because of a kid like you!

Little Cowboy
Happy Birthday little cowboy
may you have a rodeo kind of day.
Stay in the saddle and ride 'em
buckin' and broncin' all the way.

Then when your ride is over
and you're feeling tuckered out,
Listen and you'll hear the cheering
for a rodeo Happy Birthday shout!
– Sharon Ezzell

Today's your Birthday!!!
Monday's child is fair of face
Tuesday's child is full of grace
Wednesday's child is full of woe
Thursday's child has far to go
Friday's child is loving and giving
Saturday's child works hard for a living
But the child born on Sunday the Sabbath
Is boony and blith and good and gay

Co-Worker

- A cubicle is just a padded cell without a door. A birthday is just a day for everyone to be all happy about your birth!

- Beware of geeks bearing gifts.

- Hard work never killed anyone. Only too many birthdays!

- I love deadlines. I especially like the whooshing sound they make as they go flying by. Kind of like your birthday did. Whoosh!! Sorry I missed it. Happy Belated Birthday

- Scratch a dog and you'll find a permanent job. Run this card through the shredder and throw it in the air and you will have some confetti for your birthday! Have a great one! (Not responsible for the mess you make.)

- We earn a seven-figure salary and unfortunately, there's a decimal point involved. So your card is your present!

- You make each day a better day with your smile and kindness. Thank you for making the work place a friendly environment! Happy Birthday - GG Milam

- Your Birthday is a wonderful time to say "thank you" for your friendship. Blessings on your special day.

What a wonderful day for a birthday!
And how wonderful that we get to share
On your special day In a special cyber way
Blessings to my online buddy
- Thena Smith

We feel so very blessed, yes, indeed we do
To count among our friends online
A special friend like you.
- Thena Smith

Happy Birthday to our friend and best wishes for the day
To bring just the sort of fun that you're hoping for your way!
- Thena Smith

Daughter

- Daddy's Little Girl
- My Little Blessing
- My Little Princess
- My Twinkle Toes
- Pretty Princess
- To My Loving Daughter

I'm thankful the Lord gave me
You as a daughter to love

A Daughter is a joy bringer
A Daughter a heart warmer
A Daughter a memory maker
A Daughter is Love
A Daughter is You
Happy Birthday!

The Lord blessed my heart
The day He gave me you

You were once my little girl
And now my shining star
Look how big you've grown
So beautiful and sweet
You make me so proud
And I just wanted to tell you
On this your special day
How very much I love you

A Daughter is Love

A daughter is smiles
A daughter is snuggles
A daughter is smart
A daughter is thoughtful
A daughter is giving
A daughter is honoring
A daughter is wonderful
A daughter is YOU!

You're the sparkle in my eyes
The twinkle in my toes
And the kiss on my heart
You are the gift I dreamed of
All of my life over and over
Now we celebrate your birthday
As you become a young woman
No matter how old you get
You will always be my little girl
Happy Birthday Dear Daughter
– LaTourelle

My Daughter

You are a beautiful person
I want you to know that
No matter what you do,
What you think, or what you say
You will have my love forever.
Happy Birthday
– LaTourelle

The Lord sent me you to love, to hold so close.
Tears come to my eyes and to my heart each time
I look at you. You are a beautiful blessing.
Happy Birthday
– GG Milam

Dear Daughter,

You have a way about you
That's definitely your own.
I see it in so many ways...
Your thoughtfulness,
Your intuition, your smile
Your song... You are so special.
I'm proud you are mine.
I Love You
Happy Birthday
– LaTourelle

In the thoughtful things you do
And the smile upon your face
You show your love so true
With your beauty and your grace
Happy Birthday
– LaTourelle

Daughters are a blessing Especially mine!

Whatever there is in my life that's right
Without a doubt you are the best
Your light shines and lifts the hearts
Of everyone that knows you
Daughter you are love
I am so very blessed
May your cup runneth over
On this your special day
– LaTourelle

The company of you
Is all my dreams come true
May this your day be special
And fill your heart with love
Happy Birthday Dear Daughter
– LaTourelle

A Daughter is ~

Your princess
Pink petunia
Tomboy in jeans
Dreamer and schemer
Lover of life
Precious and pretty
Perfectly sweet
The love of my life
– LaTourelle

What is a Daughter?

She's a pleasure, a treasure, a comfort each day
Loving and sweet in her own special way
A daughter is you my beautiful child
For as long as I'm living my daughter you'll be
Happy Birthday
– LaTourelle

A daughter is love all wrapped up so sweet
She giggles with joy from way down to her feet
A treasure and comfort to delight every day
She fills up my life in her own special way
– LaTourelle

With each and every passing year
She grows much sweeter than before
Through every stage, through every age,
You can't help but love her more.
She's charm and beauty
Love and delight
She's the one true love
That God did right
– LaTourelle

Father

- Blessed indeed is the man who hears many gentle voices call him father! – Lydia M. Child

- Chance made you my Father, Love made you my Daddy

- Dear Dad, I loved going places with you as a little girl. You always made me feel like your little princess! – CC Milam

- Dear Dad, I'm so thankful to the Lord that He gave me you as my Father

- Dear Dad, Thank you for always making me feel like I could fly anywhere–that I could do anything. Thank you for giving me wings! – CC Milam

- Dear Daddy, I love you so much and I will always be your little girl – CC Milam

- Dear Daddy, I love you so much and when I get older, I'm going to marry you! Love, Katie

- Growing up, I always felt so safe and protected by you. Thank you for always being there for me. – CC Milam

- Happy Birthday to the Bestest Daddy in the whole world!!

- I know that you are not my real father but I'm thankful you are my Dad. Have a great day.

- I love you, Daddy

- I thank God everyday for giving me a Father–YOU!

- I was looking for the perfect card that really reflected something about the person you are, but I did not find any made with duct tape! – CC Milam

- I'm so thankful you are my Father

- May the Lord bless you today on your Birthday

- Thank you for being a gentle and loving Father!

- The voice of parents is the voice of God's, for to their children, they are heaven's lieutenants.

- To a wonderful man I call my Father

Thank you Dad for being such a wonderful role model for me to look up to. When I grow up I want to be a Godly man just like you.

— August Jones

To My Father,
Thank you for how you love your family. You have been a wonderful provider, a wonderful friend and a wonderful father. Thank you for your strength and the time you share with us. Happy Birthday

— GG Milam

Dear Dad,
I know we have had our hard times and I feel that all of that is in the past. The love and respect I have for you now seems like it has always been and I know it will always last. Love, Crystal

Dear Dad,
You and I have been round the block and back again. And through it all we found home. A love that was born in that first breath, so many years ago, is the glue that has held with unwavering strength in each moment of struggle, and is the polished finish that makes my life shine. Your unfailing love as a father, has guided me over the hills and into the valleys and out again. Too often we missed the point that we are an awesome team because we were too busy being stubborn. But now as the years have moved on, it is with the deepest awe that I realize just how wise and good you really are. And in these fleeting moments of enlightenment it is my prayer that the memories of that little girl will flood your soul and you will once again feel love.

Love, Your #1

Dad, I love you so much
You give my life a firm push
That can only come through
You and your steady hand.
Blessings on your birthday!
– GG Milam

I celebrate your birth today
And hope your wishes come true.
I thank God daily for giving me
A wonderful Dad like you!
– Thena Smith

On Your Special Day
I just wanted you to know that I
Love and respect you for the way
You take such good care of me and
Your family. I am truly blessed to
Have you as my father.
Blessings on Your Birthday!
– GG Milam

On Your Birthday Dad,
Thank you for being a great father
For the times you played with me
For the times you made me feel special
I love spending the day with just you!
Hope you have a Happy Birthday
– GG Milam

It's your birthday! Celebrate Make three wishes
Blow the candles Cut the cake Open the presents
Eat the cake Take a nap You've earned it
With all that hard work!! Happy Birthday!

Friend

- A friend is one of the nicest things you can have, and one of the best things you can be. - Douglas Pagels
- A single rose can be my garden... a single friend, my world. - Leo Buscaglia
- Friends share and friends care
- Friendship isn't a big thing—it's a million little things.
- May God look down from heaven above and bless your day with peace and love. - Thena Smith
- May you have a wonderful birthday filled with sunshine, flowers and showers of blessings. - GG Milam
- Thank you for your friendship
- The most beautiful discovery true friends make is that they can grow separately without growing apart. - E. Foley
- To my friend who is special and loved so much
- You mean so much to me

May roses kissed in sunshine
Glistening in the mornings dew
Be only half as wonderful
As the day in store for you
~ Thena Smith

Thanks for being such an awesome friend!
You are so wonderful to me and you are
Always there to listen when I need you
You really know how to cheer me up
When I am a little sad and blue
You have such a lovely smile that
Always seems to brighten my day
Thank you for our friendship
Have a Happy Birthday
- GG Milam

May your blessings be many
May your sorrows be few
May love be so special
Just like you
Happy Birthday Friend

On Your Birthday

I Love You and wish you a Happy Birthday.
If you were a flower, I'd pick you.
You are a perfect one with
A sweet fragrance.
– GG Milam

There's a miracle in our friendship
That dwells within my heart
Don't know when it happened
But I knew right from the start
The happiness you bring
Always gives my soul a lift
To me our special friendship
Is God's most perfect gift
Happy Birthday to You

Hope you have a Special Birthday
that is Special just like you!
Who would have thought that in this great big
world we would find each other???
You are the bestest friend I have ever had and
I hope we are friends forever!
Happy Birthday
– GG Milam

A birthday is a good time to remember our friends.
Come to think of it, at our age, it's good
To remember most anything at all!
Birthday Blessings!

You have always been a blessing
You have always been a dear
And you are a source of joy
That gets more special every year!
– Thena Smith

My birthday prayer for you
Is that God above would bless
Your life, your day, your very being
With peace, joy, love and happiness!
– Thena Smith

May today be the day
You dreamed of yesterday
And may it be much more.
May the joy of the happy day
Be only the beginning
Of the joy you have in store!
– Thena Smith

Hope your year is wonderful
Hope your day is bright
And that the blessings you received
Today last far into the night!

And tomorrow when you awake
May a smile form on your lips
And may not a bit of birthday cake
Settle on your hips!!!
– Thena Smith

Your friendship is dear to me.
Your friendship is true. I made this card to say,
"Thanks!" and Happy Birthday to you.
– GG Milam

Age is a matter of feeling, not of years.

Grandma

- ◉ I know I'm older now but I only wish you could hold me in your lap and sing me a lullaby. I love you, Nannie. You will always have a special place in my heart. Happy Birthday
- ◉ One of my most favorite places to be, Grandma, is where ever you are! Happy Birthday
- ◉ You spoil me rotten from head to toe and then sent me home to mom and dad and they can't spank Grandma-Ya, know! Happy Birthday from Katie

Dear Grandma,
The best present in the world is when I get to spend time with you. Grandma you're sparkly and funny and smell good, too. I just hope you know how much I love you. May this little card I made for you always remind you how special you are. Happy Birthday - LaTourelle

Dear Grandma,

In fond memories of road trips across the country.
We thought we would take you out to eat on your
special day-do you think McDonald's will take
a check?? Love you lots! Happy Birthday
- GG Milam

Dear Grandma,

I love to be in the kitchen when you are making dinner or a special treat but I love it even more when we sit down and actually eat! You are the best! Have a Happy Birthday

On Your Special Day, Memaw,
Thank you could never say enough for all that you do and all that you give to us and your family.
May you be richly blessed with love and happiness throughout all of your days! Have a Wonderful Birthday

Thank you for all the warm hugs and good advise
You have always freely given May the Lord bless
You today and every day for all the goodness
You have shared with me and with others
Bless You Grandma & Happy Birthday

Grandma's are a kid's best friend
But I'm extra lucky because
My Grandma is my best, best friend
Forever and ever.
I hope you have a birthday as terrific
For you as you are to me.
I love you, Grandma
Happy Birthday

Grandpa

- ◎ I know I'm older now but I only wish you could bounce me on your knee again and throw me in the air. I love you, Papa. You will always have a special place in my heart. Happy Birthday – GG Milam
- ◎ Grandpa's hold our hands and touch our hearts
- ◎ One of my most favorite places to be, Grandpa, is with you because you're so special to me. Happy Birthday – GG Milam

Dear Grandfather,
I love to hear all the stories you tell and how I learn so much about you and about life from them. I treasure them deep in my heart where there is only room for a special Grandfather like you! Hope You Have a Happy Birthday – GG Milam

Papa,
I love how you wrap me in your arms with a great big hug and tickle me to pieces down on the livingroom rug. You pack me around with such pride and joy and out of all that I play with, you are the best toy! Happy Birthday Papa Love, Bootsie #1

Wishing You Happiness

Thank you could never say enough for all that you do for me
and all of our family. You are a wonderful treasure, Papa, that
is really rare and very priceless. We treasure you today on
your Birthday and on every day. - GG Milam

Granddaughter

You are the joy in our heart and the apple of our eye
A ray of sun in the morning and always our sweetie pie.
You fill our lives with joy and gladness
And sometimes bring us a little sadness.
So on this special day we are sending to you a
Card full of love for all the wonderful things you do.
May You Have a Wonderful Birthday

To You, Granddaughter
With Thoughts on Your Special Day

May you always know how much you
Are loved and cherished by your family.
May you always know the sunshine and
Joy you bring with just a simple smile.
May you know that this is a special day
We remember and hold deeply in our hearts.
With Love, Always

To a Special Granddaughter

Fond memories of yesterdays past
Come flooding in as I look at you today.
Once a young child just up to my knee and now
A beautiful young lady so full of grace.
May you be blessed this day and always
with laughter, happiness, and joy.

Grandsons

Grandson it's a pleasure to
Watch you change and grow
You'll always have my love with you
No matter where you go!
Now that you are sixteen
I'm sure you're anxious to
Get your driver's license
Before the day is through
I guess you didn't know that
You've been driving for awhile
Because you've driven love into
My heart with every smile
So happy birthday grandson
May your wishes all come true
And may the road in your life
Be extra smooth for you!
– Jennifer Byerly

Grandsons are loved for many things,
For cheerful smiles and songs they sing
For bringing laughter and so much fun
Oh how we love you little one.

Dear Grandson,

You fill us with pride and place a smile in our heart
We fell in love with you right from the start!
Happy Birthday with many more memories to come

Filling us with pride and giving so much more,
Grandson you're a blessing we absolutely adore!
Happy Birthday with Love   – Thena Smith

Husband

- Baby you're not getting older-you're approaching magnificent! Have a very Happy Birthday!
- Happy Birthday to my hero in love
- Happy Birthday to the love of my life-from your Wife
- Happy Birthday to the one who rules our kingdom!
- Husband: H handsome U unique S smart B best A awesome N nice D dearest
- King for Today! May we crown you with blessings!
- This is the official "Husband of the Year" birthday award-You won! Happy Birthday!
- To my Lord Handsome from your Lady
- To the Lover of my soul

The day that we married I realized
I'd married the man of my dreams
You're there when I'm happy and smiling
Or coming apart at the seams
My darling, my best friend, my husband
It is you who first captured my heart
Hardworking, trustworthy and loyal
Nothing can tear us apart
Forgiving and loving and thoughtful
Oh how you make my heart sing!
I'll love you forever plus one day
And the joy to my life that you bring!
 - Jennifer Byerly

All perfect marriages are made up of couples who accept the fact that they have an imperfect marriage. In dreams and in love there are no impossibilities - Arnay

On Your Birthday, Dear

My gift to you on this day is simply
My heart... my love...
I give to you forever and
On this special day
You are the only love of my life.
I Love You, Happy Birthday

Dear Stephen,
May you have a wonderful day as
You reflect back on the memories
Of birthdays past and realize
Just how special you really are.

May you know that you are a
Blessing to me today and always.
May you thank the Lord for each
Year that passes and thank
Him for giving you life.
May the Lord bless you today in
A special way on your Birthday
– GG Milam

Love you Dear with all my heart and
Hope from each other we will never part.
I think of you on this special day
And hope to show you in every way
That my love is deep and my love is true.
I'm wishing a Happy Birthday to you!
– GG Milam

*Keep me as the apple of your eye, hide
me under the shadow of thy wings*

Thank You for Being a Wonderful Husband

Thank you Dear for your love
And the way you hold me close to you
Thank you Dear for the time you spend
With me and our beautiful children
Thank you Dear for the life that you
Have worked so hard for–for all of us
Thank you Dear for being you and for
The joy you bring to your family and
Friends, and for Being a Wonderful
Husband, Father, and Friend

> – GG Milam

I would live in your love as the
Sea-grasses live in the sea,
Borne up by each wave as it passes,
Drawn down by each wave that recedes:
I would empty my soul as the dreams
That have gathered in me,
I would beat with your heart as it beats,
I would follow your soul as it leads.

> – Sarah Teasdale

Some men are romantic and fly you to the moon
Others will help you and mow the yard in June
There are guys who love to dance all night
And wrap you in love and hold you so tight
But you my darling are someone so rare
Everything you do tells me you care
So today on your birthday I pray for you
Blow out the candles, may wishes come true
Happy Birthday, Honey!

Milestone
First Birthday

- A tiny cake & lots of fun–Our Little Darling is turning One!
- Bearly One year old
- Happy First Birthday to Our Little Sweetie Pie
- It's your 1st party–Let's celebrate with your very own cake!
- Kisses, hugs, diapers and pins–A new year of fun and joy begins! Come Celebrate Baby's First Birthday
- One is Wonderful
- One year old and just begun
- Share the joy–Let's have some fun! Our Little Baby is turning One!
- The BIG ONE
- Watch me party–I'll be wearing my cake–It's my big ONE!
- You're One and on the run–It's your day to have some fun!

I'm on my way! A year has past
And today I find I'm One at last!
– Thena Smith

Happy Birthday sweetheart, I can't believe you're one!
Soon you will start walking–next you'll start to run!
– Jennifer Byerly

I hold back sentimental tears at the most precious view
As my little one year old walks out of One and into Two.
– Thena Smith

My one year old daughter giggles with joy and sparkles with glee. She's sweetness and sunshine as she looks at me. One moment with her and she'll steal your heart. What a blessing she's been right from the start! Hugs and kisses with dresses and bows. She's a miracle baby every moment she grows.
– LaTourelle

My first six months I'm pleased to say
Helped me get started now I'm on my way...
I'm on my way to being One
And completing a whole year of fun!
 - Thena Smith

Happy Birthday Sweetheart, I can't believe you're One!
Now that you are walking, it seems you only run!
So here's a little present because you're extra sweet
A special pair of first shoes for those pitter-patter feet!
 - Jennifer Byerly

Joyfully giggling and sparkling with glee,
My one year old daughter smiles softly at me.
Just looking at her it's easy to see how she'll
Capture your heart and bless you completely.
 - LaTourelle

When God sends an angel to earth
We call this heavenly miracle "birth."
You grow sweeter with each passing day
How much you're loved, no words can say.
We hold your hand and you hold our heart
From the innermost tender part.
We watch you with love beyond what we've known
Amazed at what our love has sown.
This first year ends and we celebrate anew
The joy God brought us when He sent us you!
 - Thena Smith

We loved you before you were born
We waited for nine long months to see your face
And give you a long awaited first loving embrace
Now that we loved and cuddled you for a whole year today
We can hardly believe the miracle that God sent our way
You are our one year old blessing-It's true
As we celebrate your First Birthday with you!
 - Thena Smith

Thirteenth Birthday

◎ Happy 13th Birthday

◎ Happy Birthday as you enter your teens

◎ Look out world-Here I come!

◎ Teen Time

◎ Today is a special day for you as you become a teen

◎ Welcome to the Teens

◎ You're a Teeny Now

◎ You're not a kid anymore

◎ Your cool now! Can I be your friend??

This day is very special
And I'll tell you what I mean
Today you've entered something new
The beginning of your teens

Perhaps you'll pack away your dolls
Your color books and toys
Perhaps you'll start to laugh each time
You run into a boy

But either way I hope you know
No matter what you do
Age just doesn't matter
Just as long as you are you!
- Jennifer Byerly

Look at you! You are all grown up! A teenager at last!
And I sit in amazement that the time has gone so fast!
From the day I first held you and wiped baby tears away
How could the years go so quickly that brought us to this day!
I do not want to hold you back I know that you must grow
I will love you at 2 or 20, just wanted you to know!
- Thena Smith

Sixteenth Birthday

- A gift for you—A black shining Camaro. It's a Hot Wheels! I just gave you your 1st car!! Where's my hug???
- A Young Lady all grown up
- Drive carefully. It's not only cars that can be recalled by their maker.
- Happy Birthday Sweet Sixteen
- Look out! Here comes Hot Rod
- How does a car sound for your birthday?? Voorum!! Voorum!! Beep! Beep!
- If you don't like my driving, don't call anyone. Just take another road. That's why the highway department made so many of them.
- It's just that you've grown up before my very eyes You've turned into the prettiest girl I've ever seen
- No longer a child, barely a woman
- So you are turning 16—I'll be sure and stay off the sidewalks!
- Sweet Little Sixteen
- Sweet Sixteen
- Teen Driver Beware

Sweet 16 and Never Been Kissed?
Please don't look for a prince by kissing frogs!
Don't you know those things cause warts!
Hoppy Birthday!
- GG Milam

Fifteen years have come and gone
Your sixteenth year has begun to dawn
So sing with delight and dance with glee
For this is the day God gives to thee
Happy Birthday Sweet Sixteen

Eighteenth Birthday

- ◎ Age is a very high price to pay for maturity.
- ◎ Almost a Gentleman
- ◎ Almost a Lady
- ◎ Checkout time is 18.
- ◎ Cleverly disguised as a responsible adult...
- ◎ Happy birthday to an almost adult
- ◎ Have a great time turning 18! Now your parents may let you stay out until 10pm! Don't party to hardy! - GG Milam
- ◎ To a Beautiful Lady
- ◎ With maturity comes responsibility, make wise choices. You're now an adult, do something useful like go take out the trash and clean your room!
- ◎ Your day is here! A day you have been wishing for... Make your wish and blow out your candles!!

So you are turning 18...
What I wouldn't give to be 18 again!
Love your body while you still got one
Those wrinkles are just around the corner!
Happy 18th Birthday
- GG Milam

You have your life ahead of you to go and
fulfill all the dreams you have dreamed and
to achieve all the goals you have planned for.
Just remember us little people when you reach the top!
Happy 18th Birthday!
- GG Milam

Turning 18 today? Just look at you...an adult before my eyes! My, the responsibilities you have to look forward to-like paying taxes this year, still paying high car insurance, and signing up for the military! - GG Milam

Twenty-First Birthday

- A grownup is someone who suffers from responsibility-
- Congratulations! Your an adult now. Be responsible.
- Finally 21 and legally able to do everything you've been doing since you were 15!
- Legal at last-have a blast
- So you're mature now-Go get a job!
- So... You're just 3 in dog years!
- Welcome to grownup-hood!!
- Would the boy you were be proud of the man you are? – Don Drake

Twenty-Ninth Birthday

- 29 Forever!
- 29 and barely holding on
- 29 AGAIN? Talk about recycling!
- 29 and almost ancient
- Good bye youth!
- So I think I'll be 29 now and forever and ever...

Thirtieth Birthday

- 30 is not all that dreadful. You could be 40, 50, 60...
- 30, now that is half of 60!
- A third of your life is over...
- I would not say that you are old but-all your favorite songs are on the classic rock stations!!
- Thirty something
- Thirty? Heeeeeee!
- Twenty-nine plus one
- You're not 30, you're eighteen with 12 years experience

No need to be sad
Another birthday is here
I heard that your age
Is something too cheer!
'Cause you're still in your twenties
And sort of a child...
I'm trying to be kind
After all you are turning
Just twenty plus nine!
– Jennifer Byerly

I found the perfect solution for turning 30!
You see last year I had 29 put on my baseball shirt
Now I will be 29 forever!
Sorry, number is taken–you can't have it!
– GG Milam

Really, turning 29 again?
You know you can not fool me with
those burn marks on your face–
What have I told you about trying to
Iron out those wrinkles??
Happy Birthday and
Throw that iron away!
– GG Milam

May you have a lovely birthday day!
Thirty is not all that bad
May you have thirty and more to come
And stop being so sad!
Happy 30th Birthday

I'm 29 and you're not!
Have a great year!
Happy Birthday

Fiftieth Birthday

- 50 and fabulous
- 50 and full of grace
- 50 is not very old–if you're a tree!
- After Fifty it's patch, patch, patch...
- Fifty is nifty
- Forty is the old age of youth–Fifty is the youth of old age
- Glamorously Aged
- Nifty Fifty
- O.k. You still have a full deck–You just shuffle slower now
- Really?? You're 50? I thought you already went over the hill...
- You look great! Who's your plastic surgeon??
- You make Fifty look good!
- You're young for a wine.

Now that you are fifty
I wonder if you'll wish
For years that melt away like
Ice cream in a dish
But what if that meant missing
Out on the best flavors
And all the years that promise
New memories you can savor
Melting back not forward
Was never meant to be
The way that God intended
Life for you and me
- Jennifer Byerly

I recently turned fifty, which is young for a tree, midlife for an elephant, and ancient for a quarter miler, who's son now says, "Dad, I just can't run the quarter with you anymore unless I bring something to read."   - Bill Cosby

Here's to 50 years
Of living we salute.
We wish you all the best
And 90 more to boot.
 - Jennifer Byerly

Happy birthday to you
You're really on a roll!
Celebrating 50 years
Here's to 50 more!
 - Jennifer Byerly

Turning 50?
Your advanced for your age.
Oak trees in their fifties
just start turning nutty.
Have a good one!
 - CC Milam

A very special somebody
Will soon be turning fifty
We'd like to honor her because
We think she's rather nifty
So please stop by the open house
And join with everyone
To wish Annie a happy day
Of laughter, love and fun!
 - Jennifer Byerly

Since you are turning fifty
And half a century has now passed
May all the years in front of you
Pass by you half as fast
 - Jennifer Byerly

Mother

- Another word for Mother is Love
- Dear Mommy, out of all my toys in the toy box, I love playing with you the best! Happy Birthday
- God could not be everywhere and therefore he made mothers. - Hebrew Proverb
- Grown don't mean nothing to a mother. A child is a child. They get bigger, older, but grown. In my heart it don't mean a thing. - Toni Morrison
- I know I was not always an easy kid to raise but I hope you know that I love you. Always have, always will.
- I love you Mommy with all my heart
- Mom this little card was sent your way to wish you the very best and most special day! - Thena Smith
- My Best Friend
- My Favorite Shopping Buddy
- No painter's brush, nor poet's pen, in justice to her fame, has ever reached half enough to write a mother's name.
- Thank you Mom for being there for me and loving me with all of your heart.
- You're the best Mommy in the world!

When we are born, we do not have a choice in our mother.
He hand picks them especially for us.
I'm so thankful He chose you to be my mom. I love you.
- GG Milam

I remember my mother's prayers and
they have always followed me.
They have clung to me all my life.
~ Abraham Lincoln

It's your birthday Mom
And I'm sending your way
A special little card to say
That I love you above all the rest
And pray for you a day full of joy
And a life full of happiness!
– Thena Smith

Happy Birthday Mother!
If I could have chosen a mother
I would have chosen no other
Than the one I have in you
For you are wonderful
Through and through!
– Thena Smith

Mom, I love you so very much.
You gave my life a gentle touch
That can only come through
A wonderful blessing such as you!
So I celebrate your birth today
And hope your wishes come true.
I thank God daily for giving me
A wonderful Mom like you!
– Thena Smith

For a Special Mother-in-Law
You have always been a blessing
You have always been a dear
And you are a source of joy
That gets more special every year!
– Thena Smith

I love you my Mother
My friend

Now thank we all our God,
With hearts, and hands and voices,
Who wondrous things has done,
In whom His world rejoices:
Who from our mother's arms
Has blessed us on our way
With countless gifts of love,
And still is our today.
– Martin Rinkart

Mom

You've always been a part of me
Right from the very start,
Creating treasured memories
Tucked deep within my heart.
You taught me what love truly means,
I've watched your caring ways,
Unselfishly guiding me through any stormy days.
I'm thankful for the times we've shared
And look forward to the rest.
When it comes to Moms,
There is no doubt I know I have the best.

You never really understand the love of God
until you become a mother. One minute you
are so upset with your child and their actions
and the next you are embracing them in your
arms with unconditional love. This is how God
loves us. Thank you Mother for your love and
teaching me the love of God and how to live
for Him everyday of my life. I promise to pass
these truths onto my children and grandchildren.
Happy Mother's Day
– GG Milam

A Mother's Love is for Eternity

Niece

My sister gave to me
A daughter as sweet as she
With sparkling eyes
And giggles galore
What Aunt could ask
For anything more
Nieces are nice
Like sugar and spice
Nice and neat
A niece so sweet

To My Dear Niece
In God's perfect plan,
Family comes together
Not just by chance.
I'm so thankful the Lord
Gave you me as a niece.
May He bless you on your
Special day

On Your Birthday
I love you and wish you a Happy Birthday.
If you were a flower, I'd pick you.
You are a perfect one with a sweet fragrance.
– GG Milam

You have grown in to a beautiful young lady
That shines more and more each day.
I'm so proud of you and all of your accomplishments.
I am blessed to have you as my niece and my friend.
Blessings to you on your Birthday

Nephew

What a joy
My brother's boy
My brother in duplicate
God created brothers
And blessed us
With their sons
What a blessing and joy
My brother's sweet boy

What have I been doing?
Time flew swiftly by
My how you have grown
Into such a handsome guy

I have loved you as a son
And you have love me as a father.
You have brought special meaning to my life.
I'm so thankful to have you as my nephew,
My friend, and my special son.
Happy Birthday
– GG Milam

As I reflect over the years of you as a boy,
Cherished memories come to mind of the days
Teaching you to play baseball and going fishing.
I now see you sharing precious times with your
Children and I am filled with pride at the
Man and father you have become.
Today is a wonderful day to let you know you are
Loved and to wish you a Happy Birthday
– GG Milam

Over the Hill

- According to my best recollection, I don't remember.
- Age is an issue of mind over matter. If you don't mind, it doesn't matter. – Mark Twain
- Age is important only if you're cheese or wine.
- Almost Extinct!
- Ancient, Ancient, Ancient
- At my age, I've seen it all, done it all, and heard it all– I just can't remember it all.
- Birthdays are good for you–the more you have the longer you live!
- Blow torch, please!
- Born in the USA a loooooooong time ago
- Don't think of yourself as old, think of yourself as experienced.
- Eat right, exercise regularly, die anyway.
- For all the advances in medicine, there is still no cure for the common birthday. – John Glenn
- Geezer, formerly known as "Stud Muffin"
- Grow old along with me! The best is yet to be. – Robert Browning
- How old are you again? Tap your cane on the floor when I get close.
- I am long on ideas, but short on time. I expect to live to be only about a hundred. – Thomas Edison
- I heard that you are so old that you and your teeth don't sleep together anymore...
- Jurassic–Prehistoric
- Just remember, once you're over the hill you begin to pick up speed.
- Life is not measured by years, but anniversaries of the heart.

- Many of your co-workers were born the same year that you got your last promotion.
- Middle-age is when broadness of the mind and narrowness of the waist change places.
- Old age and treachery will always overcome youth and skill.
- Seems I've had a great life, but I just can't remember most of it.
- So many candles so little cake
- Some folks say 40 is over the hill. I think those folks are just a pill! For look at you—you are cool as can be and you are not forty but 43! – Thena Smith
- The older I get, the better I was.
- The older the fiddler, the sweeter the tune.
- The secret to staying young is to find an age you really like and stick with it!
- This year on your birthday your 40 years young, your life isn't over—it's barely begun! – Jennifer Byerly
- To prepare for the lighting of your candles... Everyone put on your sunglasses!
- Today is the yesterday you worried about tomorrow.
- Warning: Dates in calendar are closer than they appear.
- We would light the candles on your cake but it might set off the fire alarm and the sprinklers.
- Wrinkled was not one of the things I wanted to be when I grew up!
- You know you are getting older when there is not enough room on your cake for all the candles.
- You know you're getting older when you know all the answers, but nobody asks you the questions anymore!
- You're 60 years of age. That's only 16 Celsius!
- You're how old?? That just can't be possible...
- You're not getting older, think of it as more experienced.

Over the hill?
I think not!
You're looking good
And you've still got
Vim, vigor and zest
And as for friends
You are the best!
– Thena Smith

There's just no denyin'
When old age arrives
When stomach and chins
Take their plunging nose dive
You don't need to worry
If you're falling apart
As long as you nurture
The youth in your heart!
– Jennifer Byerly

Little jars of moisturizer sitting in a row
Lipsticks on the counter colors all aglow...
Powder and blushes, at the ready
Masks should be close as hand
Wrinkle removers at attention
Ready on demand...
Base, concealer, tweezers, pencils
Ah and a "Tricks the Stars Use" book
All necessary to achieve
That daily Natural Look!
– Thena Smith

Yes, it is getting hot in here and no,
I don't think it is your hot flashes this time.
From that blinding light, I think it is your cake!
Have a Hotty Birthday
– GG Milam

Pastor

- ◎ I call you Pastor but know you as friend. Please take this gift and love without end. - LaTourelle
- ◎ PASTOR–Another word for friend, confidant, prayer warrior, servant, teacher, preacher and man after God's own heart. – LaTourelle
- ◎ Prayer is exhaling the spirit of man and inhaling the spirit of God. - Edwin Keble
- ◎ Shepard of the Flock
- ◎ Thank you, Pastor, for showing me God's love in the way that you live from day to day. - LaTourelle
- ◎ To know you is to see the light of God's love close-up.
- ◎ When I look into your eyes I see the love that God has given me.
- ◎ Who rises from prayer a better man, his prayer is answered. - George Meredith

Dear Pastor,

Thank you for being such a blessing to our family.
You have given to our family in so many ways
Through your time, your prayers, and your heart.
Thank you for being such a wonderful man of God.
May the Lord abundantly bless you.
Happy Birthday
- GG Milam

Dear Pastor
May the Lord bless you and restore you
May He give you comfort and rest
May He guide you in His path
May He give you strength and encouragement
May He fill your life with peace and joy
May You Have a Happy Birthday

You guide us with your loving hand
And comfort us with prayer
We thank you for such dedication
Dear Pastor you are so rare
– LaTourelle

When God looks down upon his church
And hears your words and watches your care
He sees in you a man that longs to be like Jesus
What a blessing you are to us as you lead us
To a deeper understanding of what real love is
Thank you for your loving example
And for keeping us in your prayers
May you be blessed abundantly
Happy Birthday (or other occasion)
– LaTourelle

Secret Pal

To My Secret Pal

May the Lord watch over you and keep
you in all that you do throughout your day.
May He send His peace and comfort
And fill you with blessings in every way.
You're in my prayers today and always.
Your Secret Pal

May the Lord lead you and guide you
Today and everyday and in every way!
Your Secret Pal

The Lord is good. The Lord is great.
The Lord bless you this day as we celebrate.
Happy Birthday
From your Secret Pal

Sister

- A little sister is someone to look up to.
- A sister is a bit of childhood that can never be lost.
- A sister is a special kind of friend. Sisters by chance, friends by choice.
- Be kind to thy sister. Not many may know the depths of sisterly love. – Margaret Courtney
- God made us sisters, His love made us friends.
- Enchanting and sweet from your head to your feet, touching my heart–my life is complete.
- Giggles, secrets, sometimes tears–sister and friend through the years.
- I loved you too much to be your friend, so God let me be your sister.
- Secrets to whisper, memories to share, a sister's love is forever near.
- Sisters are different flowers from the same garden.
- Sisters to talk, laugh, sing and cry. God bless us so with a love 'til we die.
- There is no time like the old time, when you and I were young.
- To have a loving relationship with a sister is not simply to have a buddy or a confidant. It is to have a soulmate for life. – Victoria Secunda
- You are my sister, you are my best friend. Oh how blessed I have love without end.

Our days sipping tea and
conversation shall never end.
For though you're my sister,
you are always my friend.

You will always be my nerdy little sister
But I'm thankful I still have you
To pick on, to make fun of, to love.
I really do love you!
Happy Birthday

Nothing can compare
to the bond that we share
Forever sisters
Forever friends
Until the end

I love that you are my big sister
For you always watch out for me
You share your cool big girl stuff
You take me places with you
Even though I get on your nerves
And sometimes... you love me for me
Thank you, Sissy, and Happy Birthday

Dear Sister, Have I ever told you,
You are my best friend?

The desire to be and have a sister is a primitive and profound one that may have everything or nothing to do with the family a woman is born to. It is a desire to know and be known by someone who shares blood and body, history and dreams.   – Elizabeth Fisher

Sisters
Family
Friends
Forever
Birthday Blessings

Sister, you are the sweetness and love
Sent to me from heaven above.
On your birthday may you know
My love is with you wherever you go.
Happy Birthday

Blessings on Your Birthday
Much to the human heart's delight,
Love does indeed make all things right.
Through every joy, and any strife,
A sister is a friend for life!

Sisters are special
From young ones to old.
God gave me a sister
More precious than gold.

Happy Birthday Sister
This message comes your way
With smiles and good wishes
Upon your special day!
It's nothing all that fancy
But it's full of love for you
Here's hoping that your birthday
Is awesome just like you!
– Jennifer Byerly

S for sophisticated
I for intelligent
S for sweet
T for terrific
E for elegant
R for rare
All these things and more.
Are everything that I adore
Happy Birthday, Sister

My Sister, My Friend
You are joy without end
May your birthday be
The best it's ever been
And may you feel love
Coming down from above
Happy Birthday!

Today on your birthday I pray
Health, wealth and happiness
And all your dreams come true

With a sister you share a common history
Of all that is, and what can be.
As childhood tears and innocent fears
Melt into memory over the years

Happy Bearthday Sis,
Remember when we used to play with our teddies...
We dressed them all in their finest lace and silk,
Together we sipped tea and ate the cookies mom baked.
Oh, what fun it was to talk and laugh and be so silly.
I dream often of the times we've shared, just you and I
And I pray for the time when we shall do it once more.
My wish for you this birthday is that you will find a quiet
Place to sit with a cup of tea and in that special time you
Will remember love and the special bond we share as sisters.

Son

- A reflection of your father
- Captain of my Heart
- Dear Son, If you ever wonder, I will love you forever!
- Happy Birthday, Son!
- I'm so thankful the Lord gave me you as a son to love and cherish.
- My Little Man
- My Little Prince
- Snips and Snails and Puppy Dog Tails
- Thank Heaven for Little Boys
- That's my Boy!
- The Lord shined down upon on me the day He gave me you, a Son.
- To My Son, I love you
- To My Wonderful Son
- What a guy!
- With Pride, To My Son
- You are my "Son" shine
- You are the joy of our life.
- You're such a big boy!
- Young boys become great men. - Don Drake

Today is your day!
Let's celebrate the wonder of you—
Happy Birthday to our Son!
Only God could create a little boy
As special as you!

Look at that wonderful creature
That we call a little boy
Only God in Heaven above
Could create such a package of joy!

I remember when you were a baby
It was love at first sight from the start
Each day was like a new chapter
In a book that I store in my heart

The memories are etched there forever
Where I'll cherish them all of my days
As I've watched you grow into manhood
From the boy who was always at play

My feeling of joy runs so deeply
With the love that I feel for you son
As I've watched with pride as you've grown
Into the man that you now have become!
– Jennifer Byerly

Who would have thought of all of the things
That occupy a little boys mind?
If we were to look inside his head
What wonderful things would we find?

His imagination when let run free
Lets him wondrous things to see
And he finds joy in all manner of things
From rocket ships to tennis shoestrings!

He can love a puppy dog or a rat
With just as much ease
And when given the opportunity
A little boy loves to please.

Dear Son,
May the Lord always shine His face upon you
And bring you peace and abundant joy into your life.
I thank Him today and the day you were born.
Blessings to you today and everyday
Happy Birthday

A bundle full of goodness
Tiny trousers denim blue!
My precious little baby
Oh yes, that babe was you!

A burst of lots of energy
Running here and there
Dirty face and fingers
Disheveled, cap-worn hair

Tree climbing, laughing youngster
A noisy, busy boy
Always asking questions
A daily source of joy

Growing, changing, handsome,
Mannerly young lad
Whenever you were in my arms
It always made me glad

Maturing into someone
Of whom I'm so proud of
Although you're now a man
You're still the boy I love!
- Jennifer Byerly

Happy Birthday to a guy who's smart,
charming, and absolutely gorgeous–and
I'd say so even if I WEREN'T your mom!
- Thena Smith

To Teenage Son

Don't race the car! Don't waste gas!
Go lightly on the peddle and don't drive so fast!
Stop at lights! Drive with discretion!
Now about my other rules... Do you have a question?
- Thena Smith

There is a special bond
Between a son and his mother
It has a tenderness and uniqueness
Unlike any other
From the time he is a baby
Held in those arms so loving
He knows this love is special
Sent from the Lord above him
As a toddler and youngster he knows
That his mom is special and tries
Always to be there to console him
When she hears his cries.
A teenager's love is so special
And even though it remains unspoken
There are special cords of love
That never can be broken.
But when he suddenly becomes a man
The emotions in his heart and soul
Respond as if on remote control
And he once again feels free to express
His love and warmth and tenderness.
The bond that has been dormant
For some of those teenage years
Brings joy to his mother's heart
And can reduce her to happy tears.
And when he chooses a wife to wed
He treats her with gentleness he learned from
The one who loved him like no other
His wonderful, loving and adored mother!

      - Thena Smith

Teen

- Drive carefully–Cars aren't the only things that can be recalled by their maker!
- Happy Birthday to one cool friend. Hope you have a great– I mean cool birthday – GG Milam
- Have fun on your birthday.
- WARNING: Teenager zone. Enter at your own risk!
- You are a blessing to our family.
- You are special to me. Happy Birthday
- You are wonderful person and a great friend.

How does a car sound for your Birthday???
Honk! Honk!
Hope you have one bumper of a Birthday!
(Oh yeah! Cars have two bumpers!)
– GG Milam

So you really want to know who is on the $100 bill?
Didn't you learn that in history class?
Maybe you need to go look it up–
After you have a Happy Birthday!
– GG Milam

On Your Special Day
I'd say you can do anything your heart desires
For you are really talented and smart.
Make some plans, pick a dream
Then follow it with all your heart.
Blessings to you

Happy Birthday
To one of my most favorite people
From one of your most favorite persons

I do not want to hold you back
I know that you must grow
But be you 2 or 20
Just know I love you so!
– Thena Smith

Look at you!
You are all grown up!
A teenager at last!
And I sit in amazement
That the time has gone so fast!
From the day I first held you
And wiped baby tears away
How could the years go so quickly
That brought us to this day!
– Thena Smith

It seems like only yesterday
I held you on my lap
And then I kissed you on your cheek
As I lay you down to nap

Now you're older, things have changed
A teen you have become
But I still plan to hold you close
When each day is done

No matter what your age may be
From one to ninety nine
You'll always have a place inside
These open arms of mine
– Jennifer Byerly

You can be any one you wish to be.
Reach high, pick a star.

Teens are great
Teen years are fun
Enjoy being a teen
For you've just begun!
Thirteen is a wonderful age
And you feel so grown up too
This is a special birthday wish
Especially for you.
– Thena Smith

If I could give you diamonds
For every hug you gave to me
If I could give you pearls for
The smiles you sent my way
If I could give you sapphires
For each kindness that you gave
Then your crown would be adorned
With gems of love more precious
Than all the kingdoms jewels
May you sparkle and shine
With these gifts from my heart
Happy Birthday

This day is very special
And I'll tell you what I mean.
Today you've entered something new–
The beginning of your teens.
Perhaps you'll pack away your dolls
Your color books and toys.
Perhaps you'll start to laugh each time
You run into a boy.
But either way I hope you know
No matter what you do,
Age just doesn't matter
Just as long as you are you!
– Jennifer Byerly

Uncle

An uncle is a double blessing–
You love like a parent and act like a friend!
Thank you for being so great to me
May the Lord bless you with the
Desires of your heart on your Birthday

*I'm so glad I have an uncle like you.
You are a gift whose worth cannot be
measured except by the heart.
Happy Birthday*

An uncle is someone special
To remember with warmth,
Think of with pride,
And cherish with love.
Blessing on your Birthday

Happy Birthday Uncle Jerry
Isn't it just great how much
Talent, good looks, smarts, and
Pride can come out of one family?
Sounds like you raised me pretty good, right?
- GG Milam

Happy Birthday Uncle Troy
Thank you for all that you do for me
And how you love me as your own
I love our special relationship
Thank you could never be enough
For such a wonderful man in my life
Thank you for your love
- GG Milam

Wife

- A kiss for you my love
- A mother, a friend, the love of my life, I am so blessed to call you my wife. Happy Birthday, Darling - GG Milam
- Charm is deceptive, and beauty is fleeting; but a woman who fears the Lord is to be praised. - Proverbs 31:30 NIV
- He who finds a wife finds what is good and receives favor from the Lord. - Proverbs 18:22 NIV
- My Beautiful Lady
- The best moments of my life are with you.
- The Queen of My Heart
- Whenever I think of you and our love, I overflow inside.
- You are my wife, lover and friend, I cherish you!
- You are wonderful wife and mother.
- You touch me with your eyes, your words, your love...

To My Loving Wife
Thank you for always loving me
Even when I am hard to love
Thank you for always taking care
Of the children God sent us from above
Thank you for all the little things you do
Thank you for just being you!
Happy Birthday
- August Jones

Even though you do not hear me often say those
Three little words that mean so very much to you,
I promise with all my heart that I do Love You.
I pray your birthday is the best.
- GG Milam

My Love, My Everything

If I could take a picture
Of every smile you've had
Then surely it would serve to
Make my days all glad
I'd gaze upon your photos
Reflecting on your love
Dear wife you are surely
A gift from God above!
– Jennifer Byerly

Today is your day to celebrate
But today is my day to celebrate you
Happy Birthday to You!
Queen for a Day and My Life
Happy Birthday!

You've always been that special
Darling I adore
Your smiles and your laughter
Warm me to the core
Of this I know I'll always
Count on all my days
Sweetheart you are someone
Who sets my heart ablaze!
– Jennifer Byerly

My Woman, My Woman, My Wife
On this birthday may all your wishes come true
May God hear every prayer spoken for you
You give to our lives so much love and care
You are precious to each of us beyond compare

The Lady of my Life

At times I cannot find the words to express
the love I feel for you and the happiness
you bring to me each new shiny day
and today I wish you a Happy Birthday
 – GG Milam

Let love and faithfulness never leave you;
Bind them around your neck,
Write them on the tablet of your heart.
 – The book of Proverbs

No other woman could be so much to so many,
You touch our lives in a special way
Giving, caring and always praying
What a blessing you bring to our life
Happy Birthday My Beautiful Wife

You are the sunshine
And joy in my life
I can't imagine anyone
Who would be such a perfect wife
That's why I could hardly wait
To send a loving card your way
To tell you that I love you
And wish you the very best birthday!!
 – Thena Smith

A wife of noble character who can find?
She is worth far more than rubies.
Her husband has full confidence in
Her and lacks nothing of value.
She brings him good, not harm,
All the days of her life.
Her children arise and call her blessed;
Her husband also, and he praises her:
Many women do noble things,
But you surpass them all.
 – Proverbs 31:10-12, 28-29 NIV

Miscellaneous

- ⦿ _____ and Holding
- ⦿ A birthday is just the first day of another 365-day journey around the sun. Enjoy the trip.
- ⦿ A star danced on the night you were born.
- ⦿ Age does not make us childish, as some say; it finds us true children. - Johann Wolfgang von Goethe
- ⦿ Birth may be a matter of a moment, but it is a unique one. - Frederick Leboyer
- ⦿ Birthdays are good for you. The more you have, the longer you live.
- ⦿ Eventually, you will reach a point when you stop lying about your age and start bragging about it.
- ⦿ Grow old along with me! The best is yet to be. - Robert Browning
- ⦿ Growing old is mandatory. Growing up is optional.
- ⦿ Happy Birthday to someone with charm, grace and humor.
- ⦿ Happy Bday-You're how old? Oh, I thought you were sisters!
- ⦿ Have a Fun-tastic Birthday! If you don't it's your own fault.
- ⦿ Hey Diddle Diddle, You're older... a little!
- ⦿ I am not a has-been, I am a will be. - Lauren Bacall
- ⦿ I have liked remembering almost as much as I have liked living. - William Maxwell
- ⦿ I wanted to get you something totally impractical for your birthday, but then I realized you already have a husband.
- ⦿ I'm going shopping today for my birthday. I'm buying a new body... Size 8 please!
- ⦿ I'm not having hot flashes, just power surges.
- ⦿ In youth we learn; in age we understand.
- ⦿ Inside every older person is a younger person wondering what happened. - Jennifer Yane
- ⦿ Isn't old age fifteen years that what you really are?

- It's your birthday, do stuff you're not supposed to do.
- Let them eat cake
- Let's Party!
- Life is short—open your presents early! Have a great day and may all wishes come true.
- Make and wish and blow out your candles! Just don't pass out!
- May all your birthday dreams come true—especially the tall, dark and handsome one.
- May all your most magical wishes come true.
- May your birthday be a day to remember and filled with joy to remember always.
- Men are equal; it is not birth but virtue that makes the difference. –Voltaire
- Middle-age is when you've met so many people that every new person you meet reminds you of someone else. – Ogden Nash
- Nobility is not a birthright; it is defined by one's actions.
- Oh, No! It's the Big ___ !
- Older and Wiser
- Party, cake, ice cream, punch and YOU!
- Real birthdays are not annual affairs. Real birthdays are the days when we have a new birth. – Ralph Parle
- Roaring Twenties
- She's pretty, she's fine, but 39?
- Smile, it's your birthday! Laugh, this is your present.
- So many candles–So little cake and don't forget the ice cream!
- Some guy's got it and some guy's don't, and you're definitely one of the Got-it's!
- Sparkling Wishes
- The advantage of being eighty years old is that one has many people to love. – Renoir
- The dull, blunt needle of time sews another button on a sadly worn pair of under drawers.

- ◉ The first hundred years are the hardest.
- ◉ The old believe everything; the middle-aged suspect everything; the young know everything. – Wilde
- ◉ The secret of an enjoyable birthday can be found in achieving balance, cake, ice cream, cake, ice cream!
- ◉ The secret of staying young is to live honestly, eat slowly, and lie about your age. – Lucille Ball
- ◉ The Years tell us much that the Days never knew. – Emerson
- ◉ There comes a time when you should stop expecting other people to make a big deal about your birthday. That time is–age eleven.
- ◉ This is your special day–for special you!
- ◉ We know we're getting old when the only thing we want for our birthday is not to be reminded of it.
- ◉ When you have loved as she has loved, you grow old beautifully. – W. Somerset Mangham
- ◉ You deserve the best today… and always.
- ◉ You know you are getting old when the candles cost more than the cake. – Bob Hope
- ◉ You say it's your birthday! Well, it's my birthday, too. No, not really, I just thought it might make you feel better. – Nicocacola
- ◉ You were born an original. – John Mason
- ◉ Young at heart, slightly older in other places…
- ◉ Youth comes but once in a lifetime. – Henry Wadsworth Longfellow
- ◉ Youth has no age. – Picasso

May your day be filled with blessings,
like the sun that lights the sky,
And may you always have the courage
to spread your wings and fly!

Dear Danna,
You're 25th birthday is near
And I send this card and gift your way
To wish you a happy day

You can take no credit for
Beauty at sixteen. But if you are
Beautiful at sixty, it will be
Your soul's own doing.

May the dreams you hold dearest,
Be those, which come true,
The kindness you spread,
Keep returning to you.

Some people, no matter
how old they get,
never lose their beauty...
They merely move it from
their faces into their hearts.

Birthday Blessings for you
As you go through your day
May multiple blessings
Best sent your way.
– Thena Smith

Birthdays are a wonderful time to come to you
and let you know how special you really are.

We will not speak of years tonight
For what have years to bring but
larger floods of love and light,
and sweeter songs to sing?
– Oliver W. Holmes

If wrinkles must be written on our brows,
Let them not be written upon the heart.
The spirit should never grow old.
– Garfield

May your life be filled with everything
you have dreamed of and more.
You deserve the best!

Birthday Across the Miles
This year on your birthday
Raise your face up to the skies
And feel my love reign down as
You slowly close your eyes!

Though an ocean separates us
We still share the same sky
The same sun shines upon us
The same moon on the rise

So tonight if you should want to
Please wish upon a star
And I'll be wishing with you
Across the miles far!
– Jennifer Byerly

You are so sweet and you sharing
your birthday is such a treat.

BLESSINGS

- A blessing is a gift sent from heaven wrapped by God.
- Abundant blessings to you.
- And they shall put my name upon the children of Israel and I will bless thee. - Numbers 6:27 KJV
- Blessings come in all shapes and sizes
- Blessings to you
- Have a bright and cheery day all along your way. - GG Milam
- Let me walk beside you in sunlight or in rain. Let me share your joy and your times of pain.
- May God bless you and all you love with joy untold, As you in His arms, He enfolds.
- May the Lord bless you and hold you close to Him
- Smile, you may be a blessing to someone today!
- Stand on His promises and you will be blessed!
- Thank you for being such a blessing to me.

May you always have-
Walls for the winds,
A roof for the rain,
Tea beside the fire,
Laughter to cheer you,
Those you love near you,
And all that your heart may desire
A sunbeam to warm you,
A moonbeam to charm you,
A sheltering angel,
So nothing can harm you.
- Irish Blessing

Blessings are unexpected acts of kindness.
~ CC Milam

Blessings for you
As you go through your day
May multiple blessings
Be sent your way.
– Thena Smith

Here's a few words that best describe you
Generous, giving, kindhearted, too!
Loving and caring in all that you do
My wish is that peace would be unto you!
Blessings to you.
– Jennifer Byerly

A blessing is a gift so full of grace
Welcomed with love no matter the place.
Thank you my love for all that you are
My treasure, my love, a heavenly star.
May memory open the heart's door wide
And make you a child at your mother's side,
And may you feel her love around you
As happy memories surround you!

Dear Stephen,
The Son will always shine on you!
May the Lord bless you as you go and serve Him.
You are in our prayers and part of our hearts are there
With you as we wish we could be there too.
May you plant seeds of His love and reap a harvest of joy.
– GG Milam

The Lord bless you and keep you;
The Lord make His face shine upon
you and be gracious to you;
The Lord turn His face toward
you and give you peace.
~ Numbers 6:24-26 NIV

The Lord longs to be gracious to you;
He rises to show you compassion.
For the Lord is a God of justice.
Blessed are all who wait for Him!
– Isaiah 30:18 KJV

May Love surround you,
May faith sustain you,
May hope encourage you
Day by day.

O LORD, you have searched me and you know me.
You know when I sit and when I rise;
You perceive my thoughts from afar.
You discern my going out and my lying down;
You are familiar with all my ways.
Before a word is on my tongue
You know it completely, O LORD.
You hem me in–behind and before;
You have laid your hand upon me.
Such knowledge is too wonderful for me,
Too lofty for me to attain.

Where can I go from your Spirit?
Where can I flee from your presence?
If I go up to the heavens, you are there;
If I make my bed in the depths, you are there.
If I rise on the wings of the dawn,
If I settle on the far side of the sea,
Even there your hand will guide me,
Your right hand will hold me fast.
– Psalm 139:1-10 NIV

To be Loved by you is a Blessing!

BON VOYAGE

- A day at the beach is sand-tastic
- All Aboard
- Anchors Away
- Away we go
- Aye, Captain
- Beginning our Journey
- Choo Choo
- Come to Paradise with me
- Cruisin' Together
- First Flight
- Flyin' High
- Forecast-Sunny skies
- Full steam ahead
- Going down life's highway
- Going on a road trip
- Happy day
- Have the time of your life
- Having fun now
- Just plane fun
- Leaving on a jet plane
- Let's go play
- Let's sail away
- Many miles
- Miles of smiles with more to go
- My ship has come in
- Rolling down the rails
- Row, Row, Row your Boat
- Ships Ahoy
- Sail Away with Me
- The Great Escape
- Ticket Please
- Watching the world go by out the window

I wanted to send you on a cruise
For you being so special.
But it seems there is not enough
Green in my account.
So here is some sand and if you listen
real close to the fold in the card—
You can almost hear the ocean!

The scientific theory I like best is that the
rings of Saturn are composed entirely of lost airline
luggage. Hope you have a great trip.

A fond farewell
A hug and kisses
As you sail off
As Mr. and Misses!
– Thena Smith

Going on a trip
Going off to see
Grandma and Grandpa
And teddy is going
With me!

Wherever you go
There you are

We love you much
So please stay in touch
As you go traveling in style
And we will be waiting
When you return
To welcome you
Home with a smile!
– Thena Smith

Traveling down that long
Lonesome highway?
You're not alone
God's in the driver's seat!

Wherever you go, whatever you do, may
your guardian angel watch over you.

BREAK UP

We are never so defenseless against
suffering as when we love. - Freud

Don't cry because it's over—
Smile because it happened.

The difference between friendship and love
is how much you can hurt each other.
– Ashleigh Brilliant

A life with love must have some thorns,
but a life with no love will have no roses.

Maybe, God wants us to meet a few wrong people before
meeting the right one, so that when we finally meet
the person, we will know how to be grateful.

It's hard to tell your mind to stop loving
someone when your heart still does.

We dance to a song of heartbreak and hope
all the while wondering if somewhere and
Somehow there is someone searching for us.
– The Wonder Years

The course of true love
never did run smooth.
~ William Shakespeare

I hold it true, whate'er befall;
I feel it, when I sorrow most;
'Tis better to have loved and lost
Than never to have loved at all.
    – Lord Tennyson

I think you know how sad we are
I think you know we care
And each joy or sadness in your life
We as your best friends share.

It's hard for me to think of
The perfect words for you
To offer you some comfort
I hope you know it's true
Whenever we're together
Or whether we're apart
Thoughts and prayers for you
Dwell inside my heart
    – Jennifer Byerly

Love is a sickness full of woes,
All remedies refusing;
A plant that with most cutting grows,
Most barren with best using.
    – Samuel Daniel

And the night shall be filled with music,
And the cares that infest the day
Shall fold their tents like Arabs,
And silently steal away.
    – Henry Wadsworth Longfellow

BRIDAL SHOWER

- A cord of three is not easily broken.
- A prayer for you on your special day.
- As you go forward into the future
- Blessings today and for all the plans you have made
- Let's Shower the Bride-to-be!
- You're invited to a Bridal Shower

If it's not too hard
Please find a card
For a recipe to share
So the groom can appreciate
Meals that are first rate
From his newly married wife
Whom he has entrusted
With his well-being and life!

Cupid's work is nearly done,
Soon Lara and Nick will be 'One',
But before that Golden Hour,
We're honoring Lara with a Bridal Shower!

A sprinkle of confetti and a couple of kisses
Soon Martha and Jon will be Mr. & Mrs.
But as we wait for that special hour
Let's honor Martha with a surprise Bridal Shower!

In just a few more days,
She will gladly say, "I do"
In a white satin gown with something
Borrowed and something blue
~ CC Milam

The road is before you
As hand and hand you start
You'll travel together
One mind, one soul,
And one heart.

Come and join the celebration
In a Bridal Shower today
There will be lots of reminiscing
And fun games to play.
We know you won't want to miss it
So below is the date and time.
There will be a shower
Come rain or bright sunshine.

Today is the day she prepares for her future
As she is surrounded by family and friends.
They are helping her with gifts for her house
And with love where a home begins.
May the Lord richly bless you
Today and in the years to come.
- CG Milam

As she prepares for her home with family and friends
A part of just herself must come to an end.
She is looking towards a future with the one that she loves
And thanks the Lord in Heaven who blesses from above.
- CG Milam

A Blessing For You

May the Lord bless you and your future
May you look to Him above in all that you do
May you realize that as you both grow closer to Him
Then and only then, will you grow closer together
For a cord of three is not easily broken

BUSINESS TO BUSINESS

- Congratulations! Now you have done it again. Your even more successful and I'm so glad to call you friend!

- Friends like you are the foundation of our success, and we want you to know how much we appreciate your loyalty.

- One of the biggest thrills in life comes from doing a job well.

- Thank you for your friendship, your business, and the opportunity to serve you.

- The difference between a job and a career is the difference between forty and sixty hours a week. - Robert Frost

- The man who deals in sunshine is the man who winds the crowds. He does a lit more business than the man who peddles clouds.

- There's no business like snow business.

- We appreciate the confidence you have placed in us and we look forward to preceding you with the best possible service in the future.

- With Special Thanks and Much Appreciation

Blessings, I wish you success
Your dreams have been unlocked
You answered the door of your future
When opportunity gave a knock!
- Jennifer Byerly

To Those in the Mailroom
We're very glad that you
Take care of all the mail
All the whole year through
Thanks for all the smiles
You deliver with each letter
It always makes our work day
That much more and better!
- Jennifer Byerly

Goals

The best kind of winning takes place when
You achieve the goals that you set
By striving to do your very best
And the satisfaction from hard work you get

You aimed for the top and you made it!
And I hope that it makes you feel great
Keep up the good work and you'll be
On top every time at this rate!
– Jennifer Byerly

Don't Give Up

There's no shame to be felt when your efforts
On the top doesn't always place you
As long as you worked your hardest
At the end when each work day is through

Keep your eyes on the goal and you'll reach it
Stay focused as you hold the line!
Don't ever give up you can do it
With diligence, patience and time!
– Jennifer Byerly

Congratulations

You came each day and worked so hard
That you have earned this nice award!
If we gave out ribbons for the work you do
Your ribbon would be a wonderful shade of blue!
– Thena Smith

Your job is so important to each one of us,
You always work so diligently and never make a fuss.
You encourage other people who work with you each day,
And bring sunshine to our office in a quite delightful way!
– Thena Smith

CARDMAKER

- Beware: Cardmaker On Duty
- Cardmakers never die, they just fold-up.
- Cardmakers are creative, classy and cute.
- Cardmakers give the gift that keeps on giving.
- Cardmakers write with love.
- Cardmaking is my life, everything else is work.
- Cardmaking is my passion, but chocolate comes in a very close second!
- Cardmaking Princess
- Handmade with Love
- I'd rather be making cards.
- Silly, sassy, sentimental–cardmakers say it superbly.
- There is a very fine line between a hobby and mental illness.

If you need a poem
And you don't know where to start
Just put your pencil to the page
And write what's in your heart.
The words don't have to rhyme
And maybe they seem odd
But just write what's in your heart
And leave the rest to God.
For if he gives you the nudge to write
To console a hurting friend
Just put your pencil to the page
And the words the Lord will send.
Don't worry about what people think
About your verse or you
For God knows someone who needs
Just that word from you!
- Thena Smith

Cardmakers unite
And make people happy
With fun and laughter
Some funny, some sappy!
~ Thena Smith

If you see my wife in Wal-mart
Please send her home to me
The kids think she's been gone too long
And I'm starting to agree.
I don't know what's she's buying
Goodness knows she has it all
She bought her Christmas paper
Two years ago last fall!
She has templates, she has paper
She has eyelets, she has string
She has everything for scrapping
That could be sold to a human being!
She bought pumpkins in July
For October pages she will do
When she finishes her February pages
Of the children at the zoo!
If you see my wife in Wal-mart
She will be in a hurry I guess
And you may not be able to stop her
If she's on the way to the LSS!
- Thena Smith

Labels, tags, brads and nail-heads
I just can not get a hold
Of the newest and the trendiest—
It's gotten out of control!!

To Make a Card

To make a very special card
Isn't really all that hard–
But it takes a bit of care
To get your thoughts together
That you want to share.
Once you have a design
All settled on in your mind,
You just put it on paper
And add a poem or rhyme.
– Thena Smith

Cards for You

A tisket, a tasket
I have a whole big basket
Of lovely cards I've made today,
Ready to be sent on their way!
I've birthday cards and get well wishes
With pictures of kitties and doggies and fishes
With candies and apples and waterfalls, too,
Lovely little cards that I think will cheer you!
– Thena Smith

I like to make cards as a hobby
Though my family just claims that I'm sick,
'Cause I'm buried in items for crafting
From my toes to the top of my neck.
I own an embosser and light box,
Ribbons and markers galore,
Cardstock in every color,
Like Mulberry paper and more...
I've bought every scissor and die-cut
Adhesive? Yes, I have all kinds!
But my husband claims, all that I have
Is a bad case of losing my mind!
– Jennifer Byerly

Want to know a sure fire way
To make somebody grin?
Make a special card and then
Send it off to them.
I guarantee that it will be
The highlight of their day,
'Cause what could be much better than
A card that's been homemade.
– Jennifer Byerly

We cardmakers are a special breed,
Unique in what we do.
For it is our delight,
Morning or night,
To create special cards for you.
Poets are a special group
Who share this love so willingly.
For without lovely verses to put inside
Where would we cardmakers be?
– Thena Smith

The Perfect Card

I just made the perfect card.
It was a sight to see.
Everything was created with love
And fit so very perfectly!
The front was just beautiful
And the back was signed with care.
And in the middle was the perfect
Verse that I wanted to share.
I put it in an envelope
And sent it on it's way
Hoping that you will get it
Tomorrow or today!
– Thena Smith

ChiLDREN

- Always kiss me goodnight

- Children are magicians who make grownups smile.

- Children make days shorter, nights longer, home happier and love stronger.

- Children will soon forget your presents. They will always remember your presence.

- Daddy fly me around the moon again.

- Dance yourself silly.

- Did you ever notice that a human baby doesn't walk until it's tall enough to reach a parent's hand?

- Free hugs and giggles. Anytime!

- Happy is the son whose faith in his mother remains unchallenged. - Louisa May Alcott

- Her children arise up, and call her blessed. - Proverbs 31:28 NIV

- I remember my mother's prayers and they have always followed me. They have clung to me all my life. - A. Lincoln

- I'm growing up! Look at me! I'm bigger than I used to be!

- Mommy your hugs last long after you let me go. Love, Nat

- My mother had a great deal of trouble with me but I think she enjoyed it. - Mark Twain

- One of the most delightful sounds is that of children playing. - CC Milam

- Playing happily ever after...

- Someday, you just have to be the princess you really are.

- Sons are a heritage from the LORD, children a reward from him. - Psalms 127:3 NIV

- The sole purpose of a child's middle name is so he can tell when he's really in trouble.

- Train a child in the way he should go, and when he is old he will not turn from it. - Proverbs 22:6 KJV

I Love God
God Loves me
God bless my family
God bless me

There is a garden in every childhood,
an enchanted place where colors are brighter,
the air softer, and the morning more
fragrant than ever again.
– Elizabeth Lawrence

O ye loving mothers, know ye that in God's sight the
best of all ways to worship Him is to educate the children
and train them in all the perfections of humankind;
and no nobler deed than this can be imagined.

You came and you took... You took time and energy...
Time and attention... time and love...
Time and elbow grease... time and my sleep...
But you brought more... You brought sunshine and bubbles...
Music and laughter, sandboxes and play dough...
Yellow ribbons and flesh-colored band aids, skates
And The Waltons, and horses, and bikes and joy...
You were the best investment I ever made...

Love the Lord your God with all your heart and with
all your soul and with all your strength. These
commandments that I give you today are to be
upon your hearts. Impress them on your children.
Talk about them when you sit at home and when you walk
along the road, when you lie down and when you get up. Tie
them as symbols on your hands and bind them to your
foreheads. Write them on the doorframes of your houses
and on your gates.   – Deuteronomy 6:5-9 NIV

Chocolate

- A chocolate a day keeps the blues away.
- Best friends and chocolate go great together.
- Friends are the chocolate chips of life.
- Give me chocolate or give me death, for to live without chocolate is not living!
- God sends no stress that prayer and a bar of chocolate cannot handle!
- Hand over the chocolate and no one gets hurt.
- I am a woman of many rare moods, and they all require chocolate.
- I eat anything as long as it is chocolate.
- I never met a chocolate I didn't like.
- I only eat chocolate for you, so there will be more of me to love.
- I'd stop eating chocolate, but I'm no quitter.
- If at first you don't succeed, have a chocolate!
- If God had meant us to be thin, He would NOT have created chocolate.
- If it's chocolate–it's sending out messages for me to eat it.
- If the world was fair, clothes would wash themselves, chocolate would not be fattening and men would give birth to babies.
- If you can't eat all your chocolate, it will keep in the freezer. But if you can't eat all your chocolate, it may be a sign of a deeper problem.
- In heaven, chocolate has no calories and is served as the main course.
- Inside some of us is a thin person struggling to get out, but she can usually be sedated with some chocolate.
- It's never too early or too late for chocolate.

- Love is chocolate all wrapped up in a bite size package.
- Make mine chocolate!
- Man cannot live on chocolate alone, but women can.
- Men are like a box of chocolates. You never know when you're going to get a nut.
- Milk chocolate is a dairy product.
- Money can't buy love, but it can buy chocolate.
- One of life's mysteries is how a two-pound box of candy can make a person gain five pounds.
- Problem: How do you get a pound of chocolate home from the store in a hot car? Solution: Eat it in the parking lot.
- Promise me anything, but give me chocolate.
- Put "eat chocolate" at the top of your list of things to do today. That way at least you will get one thing done.
- Q: How many calories are there in a piece of chocolate? A: Who cares?
- Question: Why is there no such organization as Chocoholics Anonymous? Answer: Because no one wants to quit.
- S.O.S. Need chocolate!!
- Save Earth. It's the only planet with chocolate.
- So much chocolate. So little time!
- Some things in life are better rich... chocolate, coffee, chocolate, men & chocolate...
- Store your chocolate on top of your tallest cabinet. Calories are afraid of heights and will jump out of the chocolate to protect themselves.
- The best things in life are chocolate.
- The calories in white chocolate are negative and cancel out the positive calories in dark chocolate.
- The key to my heart is chocolate.
- The preservatives in chocolate will make your skin smoother and you will look younger.

- The way to a woman's heart is through a box of chocolates.
- There's nothing wrong with me that a little chocolate won't cure.
- Things are bad. Send chocolate!
- Those who say, "Nothing tastes as good as thin feels," haven't tasted chocolate!
- Warning! Chocoholic in Residence.
- Warning! I have PMS and I'm all out of chocolate!
- What is life without chocolate?
- Whatever the question is, the answer is chocolate.
- What?? You ate all the chocolate? To the store now!
- We shouldn't let a little piece of chocolate come between friends... Hand it over!
- When life gets you down and nothing is going right, you always have a friend... in chocolate.
- When my time is up, let it be death by chocolate.
- When the going gets tough, the tough get chocolate.
- Who says chocolate isn't a food group!!
- Why fall in love? I'd rather fall in chocolate.
- Will do anything for chocolate!
- You are some chocolate-bunny special.
- You are the best friend that I ever had. You're always there for me... Well maybe, my chocolate is a better friend.

Dear Lord: So far today, I am doing all right. I have not gossiped, lost my temper, been greedy, grumpy, nasty, selfish, or self-indulgent. I have not whined, moaned, cursed, or eaten any chocolate. I have not charged on my credit card. However, I am going to get out of bed in a few minutes, and I will need a lot more help after that. Amen

CHRISTMAS

- ◉ Believe and you will find Christmas.
- ◉ Christmas brings out the child in all of us.
- ◉ Christmas memories with family
- ◉ Don't go under the mistletoe with anyone else but me.
- ◉ Glory to God in the highest, and on earth peace to men on whom His favor rest. – Luke 2:14 NIV
- ◉ God grant you the light in Christmas, which is faith.
- ◉ Hang a shining star upon the highest bow.
- ◉ Hark! The Herald Angels Sing!
- ◉ Have a twinkle, jingle, ringy ding ding Christmas.
- ◉ Have yourself a Merry little Christmas.
- ◉ He is the King of Kings and Lord of Lords!
- ◉ In the hearts of children, Christmas is family and love.
- ◉ In the light of the twinkling tree
- ◉ It's beginning to look a lot like Christmas.
- ◉ Jesus is the BEST gift!
- ◉ Jesus loves you snow much!
- ◉ Jesus was born to die for your sins and bring you life!
- ◉ Let us get back our childlike faith again. – Grace Noll Crowell
- ◉ Let's put CHRIST back in CHRISTmas.
- ◉ Love was born on Christmas day.
- ◉ May the joy of the holidays fill your hearts.
- ◉ Merry Christmas to all and to all a goodnight!
- ◉ Merry Wishes and Santa's Kisses
- ◉ Oh, Little Town of Bethlehem
- ◉ Peace on earth... goodwill to you all.
- ◉ Ring the bells for Christmas in honor of His birth. Let's celebrate the moment God's son was born on earth! – J. Byerly

◉ Ring the bells, its Christmas!

◉ Silent Night, Peace on Earth with You and Yours

◉ Silver bells are ringing, the air is filled with cheer, hearts return for Christmas, my favorite time of year! - Jennifer Byerly

◉ Snowflakes are one of nature's most fragile things, but just look what they can do when they stick together. - Vesta Kelly

◉ Snowmen fall from Heaven, unassembled.

◉ Somehow, not only for Christmas, but all the long year through, the joy that you give to others, is the joy that comes back to you. - Whittier

◉ The holy star shines bright for us, that we may find the love of Christmas.

◉ The ornaments of our home are the friends that gather there.

◉ The rooms were very still while the pages were softly turned and the winter sunshine crept in to touch the bright heads and serious faces with a Christmas greeting. - Louisa May Alcott

◉ To My Santa-from the Mrs.

◉ Today in the town of David a Savior has been born to you; He is Christ the Lord. - Luke 2:11 NIV

◉ What greater joy can warm the soul of any common man? Then all the joy at Christmas time when hearts go home again. - Jennifer Byerly

◉ What joy we feel at Christmas time when we are at home! It's where we feel the happiest no matter where we roam! - Jennifer Byerly

◉ When you wish upon a star-Choose Jesus!

◉ Wishing you a holiday of love

◉ Wishing you a joy filled Christmas

Candles and stars and Christmas tree lights,
Twinkle and glow in the velvet night.

Happy Christmas Anniversary

How wonderful to know that
Since you both proclaimed "I do"
50 years have now gone by
And love still lives in you
Your union was a symbol
That God is in all things
From a lowly stable
To a wedding ring
That's why your wedding day
Was more special then the rest
You chose the day that Christ was born
Your marriage thus was blessed!
– Jennifer Byerly

Come sit at my table and share with me, warm gingerbread cookies and cinnamon tea, just you and me!

Our hearts grow tender with childhood memories and love of kindred, and we are better throughout the year for having, in spirit, become a child again at Christmastime.
– Laura Ingalls Wilder

Christmas Eve was a night of song that wrapped itself about you like a shawl but it warmed more than your body, it warmed your heart, filled it, too, with a melody that would last forever.
– Aldrich

Are you going home for Christmas? Have you written you'll be there? Going home to kiss the mother and to show her that you care? Going home to greet the father in a way to make him glad? If you're not I hope there'll never come a time you'll wish you had. Just sit down and write a letter–it will make their heartstrings hum with a tune of perfect gladness–if you'll tell them that you'll come.
– Edgar Guest

A Christmas Prayer

I pray your heart is merry
I pray your joy is bright
Throughout this special season
Of peace and hope and light!
– Jennifer Byerly

Christmas is here!
Well, almost
Not entirely here,
But awfully close!
The packages are wrapped
And under the tree
I've spotted the ones
That are for me!
– Thena Smith

God bless the master of this house,
The mistress also,
And all the little children,
That round the table go,
And all your kin and kinsmen
Than dwell both far and near;
I wish you a Merry Christmas
And a Happy New Year
– Traditional from England

The merry family gatherings–
The old, the very young;
The strangely lovely way they
harmonize in carols sung.
For Christmas is tradition time–
Traditions that recall
The precious memories down the years,
The sameness of them all.
– Marshal

God bless you in this season
of peace and hope and light
May your heart be merry
and may your joy be bright
- Jennifer Byerly

*Christmas comes but once a year
May this card bring joy and cheer
Hope your days are cheery and bright
Lift your hearts Look up tonight*

On my Christmas tree, hangs a
Picture of Grandma and me.
Her smile's so sweet
And her heart's so big.
She loves to bake bread and cookies
And fills up my tummy with treats.
Every night I thank the Lord
For giving her to me.

Family Christmas Tree

I opened the box marked Christmas
Getting ready to trim the tree
As I took each ornament out
I held an old memory

There's a Santa that belonged to Father
When he was a just a little boy
And snowflakes made by Grandma
That fill the room with joy

Bright red bows and silver bells
That take their place on the side
As children's pictures in egg carton frames
Will be displayed right in front with pride

A Christmas Invitation

You are cordially invited to a
Birthday Party of Love
GUEST OF HONOR: Jesus Christ
DATE: Today or any day—
Traditionally, December 25
TIME: Now is the time
PLACE: In your heart—
He'll meet you there,
just ask Him to come in
RSVP: He must know ahead,
so He can reserve a spot
for you at the table and
in His Invitation Book
PARTY GIVEN BY: His Children
Hope To See You There!
Let us rejoice and be glad!
Please invite your friends to come
and join in the celebration of Love
– Revelation 19:7-9

In those days Caesar Augustus issued a decree that a census should be taken of the entire Roman world. And everyone went to his own town to register. So Joseph also went up from the town of Nazareth in Galilee to Judea, to Bethlehem the town of David, because he belonged to the house and line of David. He went there to register with Mary, who was pledged to be married to him and was expecting a child. While they were there, the time came for the baby to be born, and she gave birth to her firstborn, a son. She wrapped him in clothes and placed him in a manger, because there was no room for them in the inn. – Luke 2:1, 3-6 NIV

Twas The Day Before Christmas

It was the day before Christmas while at the store
The isles were crowded making shopping a chore
When a man started yelling right at my face
It seemed to upset him, I got his parking place

The clerk said, "Merry Christmas," but I could feel
That the words she were saying weren't so real
Out of money, but still room in Santa's sack
I pulled out my plastic and continued to pack

There was pushing, shoving and rude dirty looks
The warning on T.V. said, "Look out for crooks,"
Our children must have the most on the block
It made no difference, if we went into hock

Then on a shelf that was almost picked clean
There all alone stood a Nativity Scene
I looked at baby Jesus from the land of Galilee
There were no lights, decorations or even a tree

I thought of the wise men who traveled so far
To find the baby Savior they followed a star
There in a manger in a stable so cold
Was the greatest story that was ever told

I remembered our Lord, The King of all kings
I thought of Christmas and what it really means
I looked around at the faces wanting more
Put my cards in my pocket and walked out the door.

                                            - Barbara K. Cox

The Christmas Message

There's a chill in the air and the sweet smell of pine
Friends coming together it's Christmas time
Children playing with sleds on the new fallen snow
Toys in store windows have their eyes all aglow
Chapel bells ringing from the old town square
Decorations on main street being put up with care
Christmas shoppers beginning to fill the malls
Where trees are adorned with garland and balls
Out Christmas shopping I spotted a sign
"Santa's workshop" with children waiting in line
I walked up much closer so that I could hear
What the children wanted from Santa this year
When from in line I saw a young lad
By the look on his face, he was troubled and sad
I walked nearer yet so that I could see
As he took his turn upon Santa's knee
Santa, I don't want any toys under the tree
All I want is my Daddy here with Mommy and me
It's been so long since he's been gone
When he left the grass was still green on the lawn
You see, we're in the Military and he had to go
And Mommy and I miss him more than you know
When I'm in bed and she thinks I'm asleep
She reads over his letters and starts to weep
But if you can't do it Santa, I'll understand
Since Daddy's been gone, I'm Mom's little man
As you deliver your presents give a message from me
We gave up Christmas with Daddy so children stay free.
– Barbara K. Cox

Christmas in Other Languages

Afrikander - Een Plesierige Kerfees
Argentine - Feliz Navidad
Armenian - Shenoraavor Nor Dari yev Pari Gaghand
Brazilian - Boas Festas e Feliz Ano Novo
Chinese - (Mandarin) Kung His Hsin Nien bing Chu Shen Tan
Danish - Gldelig Jul
Dutch - Vrolijk Kerstfeest en een Gelukkig Nieuwjaar!
English - Merry Christmas
Finnish - Hauskaa joulua
French - Joyeux Noel
German - Froeliche Weihnachten
Greek - Kala Christouyenna!
Hawaiian - Mele Kalikimaka me ka Hauoli Makahiki ho
Hebrew - Mo'adim Lesimkha Chena tova
Hungarian - Kellemes Karacsonyi unnepeket
Icelandic - Gledileg Jol
Indonesian - Selamat Hari Natal
Iraqi - Idah Saidan Wa Sanah Jadidah
Irish - Nodlaig mhaith chugnat
Italian - Buone Feste Natalizie
Japanese - Kurisumasu Omedeto
Norwegian - God Jul Og Godt Nytt Aar
Philippines - Maligayang Pasko
Polish - Wesolych Swiat Bozego Narodzenia
Portuguese - Boas Festas
Romanian - Sarbatori vesele
Russian - Pozdrevlyayu s prazdnikom Rozhdestva is Novim
Samoan - Maunia Le Kilisimasi ma Le Tausaga Fou
Scottish - Nollaig Chridheil agus Bliadhna Mhath Ur
Serb-Croatian - Sretam Bozic Vesela Nova Godina
Spanish - Feliz Navidad
Swedish - God Jul and (Och) Ett Gott Nytt Ar
Vietnamese - Chu'c Mu`ng Giang Sinh
Welsh - Nadolig Llawen
Yugoslavian - Cestitamo Bozic

Dear Santa

Dear Santa,
Is it true that you have jelly in your belly?
Love, Nattie

Dear Santa,
I promise I've been good and if you think I haven't,
it was all my sister's fault
Love, Katelyn

Dear Santa,
You sure do look like my Grandpa, but that's o.k., because he's
the best guy. I love him and I love you, too. Could you bring
me a saddle for the pony Grandpa made me that he thinks I
don't know about? I'll be having sweet dreams until you come.
Giddy up and fly, Love, Koby

Dear Santa,
Did you know why Christmas is so special? Well, God gave me
the best present of all, His son, Jesus. I know you can't top
that, but did you get my list of wishes?
I'll be Your little man, Alex

Dear Santa,
Mom says I've been naughty, but you know I'm really nice. Oh,
what's a girl to do? We just like to figure stuff out by ourselves. We don't mean to get into trouble, it just happens.
Anyway, I'm thanking you ahead of time for coming to my
house. You will, won't you?
Love, Cheryln

Dear Virginia,
Yes, there is a Santa Claus. Thank you for writing.
Merry Christmas, The Sun

Dear Santa,
Umm, I have to tell the truth, I really haven't been that good, but I'll bake you some really big cookies. Oh, and forget the milk, I'm leaving you hot chocolate, so you can stay warm. Does this help?
Your friend, Olivia

Dear Santa,
Girls just wanna have fun. And more fun and more fun. Sometimes we just get carried away and then mom gets mad. I guess she's too old to see we were just playing. But you know don't you? Can't wait to see you. Maybe you could tell her to pretend she didn't see us.
Hugs and Cookies, Anna

Dear Santa,
I just want you to know that I don't really need anything, so if you could just take my presents to someone who doesn't get much for Christmas, that would be the best present ever. Knowing that somewhere, some kid is happy on Christmas morning is the biggest blessing.
Your friend, Kasara

Dear Santa,
Did anyone ever tell you that red is my favorite color? You wear it so well. But that beard! Has anyone ever asked if they could give you a makeover? Well, I'm learning all this new stuff watching my mom do hairstyles on her customers. I bet I could make you look totally cool. Just think about it, maybe that could be my Christmas present to you. Oh, and this year, instead of the usual milk and cookies–I'm giving you gourmet peanut butter and jelly sandwiches and some mocha java. Maybe it'll help you stay awake better. I saw the recipes on that Good Thing show I watch. Hope you like it.
To the new you, Hannah

CONFIRMATION

May joy and happiness fill your heart
And may this day set you apart
With honor to our God above
May you feel His presence and His love
— Thena Smith

On this day as you seek to grow
And more about your God to know
May you hear His voice as He speaks to you
And to His commandments always be true

Today and Always

May you choose God before all others.
May you choose love and honor, too.
May the choices you make each and
Everyday, reflect God's love for you.

To watch you as you grow in faith
will be my greatest reward
May you always feel God's love and mercy
in your journey with the Lord

May the God of hope fill you with all joy and peace
As you trust in Him, so that you may overflow
With hope by the power of the Holy Spirit.
— Romans 15:13 NIV

May the love of Jesus Christ be with you,
guiding you every day of your life.

CONGRATULATIONS

◎ Best Wishes

◎ Best wishes on your happy occasion

◎ Blessings to you on your new adventure

◎ Congratulations on a job well done

◎ Congratulations on your new job promotion

◎ Enjoy your retirement. Congratulations!

◎ Good for you

◎ Happy, Happy, Happy for you!

◎ Many Happy Returns

◎ Nice Job

◎ No one deserves this more than you!

◎ The talent of success is nothing more than doing what you can do well and doing well whatever you do. - Longfellow

◎ Warmest congratulations to you & best wishes for the future

◎ Way to go at stepping out and making your dreams come true!

◎ We are so proud of your accomplishments

◎ Well done!

◎ You are doing great!

◎ Your accomplishments are wonderful and all that hard work is paying off! Thanks for all you do.

*Congratulations on your success!
May God bless you as you grow and
continue to use the talents and
gifts He has given you.*

DEPRESSION

- Believe you can and you're halfway there. – Theodore Roosevelt
- Hope is the thing with feathers–that perches in the soul and sings the tune without the words and never stops–at all. – Emily Dickinson
- Hope your day gets better and you will be feeling on top of things soon.
- I am with you always. – Matthew 28:20 KJV
- I can do all things through Christ which strengtheneth me. – Philippians 4:13 KJV
- In the 60's people took acid to make the world weird. Now the world is weird and people take Prozac to make it normal.
- Life is meant to be lived. – Eleanor Roosevelt
- Love is what will carry you through these difficult times. Please know there are those here who will hold you up for as long as you need. Just hold out your hand and know that we are here.
- Praise be to the God and Father of our Lord Jesus Christ, the Father of compassion and the God of all comfort, who comforts us in all our troubles, so that we can comfort those in any trouble with the comfort we ourselves have received from God. – II Corinthians 1:3-4 NIV
- When words become meaningless, please know, you are in my prayers and ever so close to my heart.
- When you look to the sky, know this: there are more stars shining inside of you than in all of the heavens above. – Lydia Garfield
- You gain strength, courage and confidence by every experience in which you really stop to look fear in the face. – Eleanor Roosevelt
- You must do the thing you think you cannot do. – E. Roosevelt
- When you feel all is lost and you can't go on, Cry out to Him. He is just a prayer away.

It Will Be Okay

When times are tough and feelings are strong,
And sometimes you think that you just can't hold on,
Remember this each and everyday,
It will be okay...
When tears seem to fall without trying at all,
And you feel that you fail when you give it your all,
Pray for this each and everyday,
It will be okay...
When pain becomes a daily feeling,
And you ask God to help you at your bedside,
kneeling, Just ask for him to say,
It will be okay...
When sadness seems hopeless to overcome,
And all you think about is how you hurt someone,
Just have faith, stand up and say,
It will be okay...
When troubles are knocking at your door,
And you wish they'd go away and be no more,
You have to think of it this way,
It will be okay...
When there's ups and downs, but more downs than ups,
And your heart often feels like an empty cup,
Always remember it this way,
I love you...
and it WILL be okay.

Although I haven't always
Had the words to give to you
To offer up some comfort
I hope you know it's true
Whenever we're together
Or whether we're apart
Thoughts and prayers for you
Dwell inside my heart
- Jennifer Byerly

I know that times are difficult
And life seems very hard
But in the midst of trials
Our strength is so revealed
A hand is there to hold you
With a love like none before
So trust and seek the wisdom
That will guide you ever on.

Did anyone ever tell you
How special you are?
Did anyone ever tell you
Just how much that they love you?
Did anyone ever tell you
How important you make others feel?
Well, someone is now and that someone is me.

Sometimes we all need something
To help us through the day
That's why I thought this candle
Might help to light the way
God cares about your sorrows
He cares about your fears
He cares about your pain and
He numbers every tear
So when you burn this candle
Let it serve to remind you
That God will always be there
To light the way for you
– Jennifer Byerly

Thinking of you today...

"Oh God!" is what I cried out
As I fell to my knees.
"I can't do it any longer
Can you help me please?"
"I need you," I continued.
"Where did I go wrong?"
"My child," He then answered.
"I've been here all along."
Then suddenly I realized
His love for me was true.
I felt my sorrows lifting
And then my burdens too.
       – Jennifer Byerly

Thank You Friend,

Thank you friend for reaching out to me at a time in my life
when it was hard for me to see. My days and nights were
blurred and I was so longing for some sleep. My house was
piling all around me for it was so hard for me to keep.

I found it such a struggle to make it through each day and
then the Lord sent an angel, He sent you my way! You listened
to by babble and help me face my fears. You reached out to
me when I needed and you wiped away my tears.

I thank the Lord for you.

You are a ray of His Sonshine that He has sent my way.
I thank the Lord for our friendship. I thank Him everyday!
– by Crystal Jones in Honor of Carol Tribou April 5, 2005

The Lord sent an angel, He sent you my way!

DIVORCE

Marriage is wonderful
And lovely for some
But there are times
When the end of marriage comes.
Divorce isn't a happy thing
For a couple to have to do,
But we want you to know
That we are here for you.
– Thena Smith

Weddings are the start
Of a journey of the heart,
But some times the journey ends
And a couple needs the
Loving support of their friends.
– Thena Smith

Here for You

Divorce hurts us deep inside
Please do not go and hide
We are here for you if you need a hug
We are here for you when you need to cry
For we are your friends forever
And that friendship will never die
– Thena Smith

I do not have the words to
Comfort you at this time.
Only my prayers and just being
Here to lend you my shoulder.
– GG Milam

One door opens and another closes

Easter

◎ Easter Greetings

◎ Easter is God's promise that He loves us one and all, He gave His Son to live for us and bids us hear him call.

◎ Easter is Here! It's time to cheer!

◎ Easter traditions with you

◎ Going on a hunt

◎ Good things come in small sugarcoated packages.

◎ Having an Egg-stremely fun time

◎ He is Risen! Just as He said! Hallelujah!

◎ He Lives!

◎ Hippity Hoppity

◎ Hopping down the Bunny Trail

◎ In your Easter bonnet with all the frills upon it, you'll be the grandest lady in the Easter Parade.

◎ Jesus died for you so you may have life eternal.

◎ May your treasure this Easter be a new life in Jesus.

◎ Our Risen Lord and Savior

◎ Rules at Easter: Don't put all your eggs in one basket. Keep your paws off other people's jelly beans.

◎ Somebunny loves you

◎ Spring is in the air!

◎ There no business like bunny business.

◎ Today is a special day of love

◎ Today is Easter–It's a Special Day to enjoy our family and with eggs play!

◎ You're no bunny 'til somebunny loves you!

Our Lord has written the promise of the resurrection not in books alone, but in every leaf in springtime.
~ Martin Luther

177

Why We Celebrate Easter

He had the power to change things that day.
He had the power to say there's no way
I'm going to hang on that cross and die.
Why should I suffer when it is not I
Who turned from my Father to bow before gold?
Who places their trust in what is lifeless and cold,
Who does not believe that I am God's Son,
That my name is Jesus that I am the One.
Why should I care what their future may be?
I'm not one of them it doesn't matter to me.
But His Father had sent Him, and He chose to obey,
So he went to the cross and died there that day.
He accepted the crown of thorns on His head,
The nails in His hands and the lies that were said.
He died so that people would truly know,
That He was God's Son as He had told them so.
He paid the price of everyone's sin,
Even of those who had killed him.
But death was no victor not then or not now,
For the tomb couldn't hold Him, the stone rolled away somehow.
He arose from the dead and walked among men
He talked, and He waited, then revealed Himself again.
To those who were doubtful or would not believe,
He showed His nail prints, the doubts to relieve.
Then He joined His Father in heaven above,
To wait for us there, to accept His love.
Yes, He had the power to change things that day,
But instead He willingly chose to obey.
He chose death on the cross, His life He did give,
So that we could believe, and in Him we could live.
Now I'm thankful to God, for sending His Son,
And I'm thankful to Jesus, for what He has done.

                                        – Sharon Ezzell

This year on Easter morning
At the rising of the sun
I'll rest my soul in Jesus
Who is the Risen One
And as the day moves forward
I'll feel the joy within
God made good on His promise
And rescued me from sin
And when the evening shadows
Are followed by the night
I'll feel the peace of Jesus
Who is my inner light!
                        - Jennifer Byerly

Tomb, thou shalt not hold Him longer;
Death is strong, but Life is stronger;
Faith and Hope triumphant say
Christ will rise on Easter Day.
                        - Phillips Brooks

But He was pierced for our transgressions,
He was crushed for our iniquities;
the punishment that brought us peace was upon Him,
And by His wounds we are healed. - Isaiah 53:5 NIV

Today is a day to reflect on all the Lord has given to us.
He gave His Son and He has given us a wonderful family.
The Lord has blessed us with so many great things! Today
we come together to praise His name!   - GG Milam

Easter is a time for us to celebrate! Jesus
Rose as promised on this special date
Along with that it brings us a special peace within
In death there are no losers if we let the Savior in
This world has confirmation God's promises are real
Because the tomb was empty Christ's rising sealed the deal!
                        - Jennifer Byerly

EMPTY NEST

Home is where your heart is until it goes off to college

Memories of our children's laughter
Pictures of them on our walls
It seems like it was only yesterday
When our children were so very small

Now that they're grown we may miss them
And the sounds of their pit patting feet
But we're proud of the adults they've become
And our job raising them is complete!
– Jennifer Byerly

The day is coming and it is very soon...
When you will walk out the door...
It doesn't seem possible that you are not
Our little girl any more. You are going off
To college and out of our home you will go...
On a brand new adventure of your own.
We love you and we are so proud of you!
– GG Milam

Why is it that a child enters your home and for the next
twenty plus years makes such a racket that you think
you are going crazy, and then, when the child departs
on his own life outside your home, the house
becomes silent and you go crazy again?
– GG Milam

Adolescence is perhaps nature's way of preparing parents to welcome the empty nest.
~ Karen Savage

My nest is empty
Where did they go?
It's too quiet now
I miss them so.

The years flew by—
We had such fun.
I love my children,
Where have they gone?

They're off to college
And working, too.
My children are grown
What shall I do?

I'll take some naps
And clean my home,
Plant a garden
And wonder some.

Yes, life is quiet
And I'll just take a rest,
For soon my grandkids
Will come visit my nest.
    – LaTourelle

With wonderful children
You were blessed
But enjoy the freedom now
Of an empty nest.

Go and visit when you want
And stay a little while
Always visit just long enough
That you leave them with a smile!
    – Thena Smith

ENCOURAGEMENT

◎ A hug is a great gift. One size fits all. It can be given for any occasion and it's easy to exchange.

◎ All I have seen teaches me to trust the Creator for all I have not seen. – Ralph Waldo Emerson

◎ All people smile in the same language.

◎ Always remember you're unique, just like everyone else.

◎ Always take time to stop and smell the roses... and sooner or later, you'll inhale a bee.

◎ Be patient. God is not finished with you yet.

◎ Be still and know that He is God.

◎ Do not wish to be anything but what you are, and try to be that perfectly. – St. Francis de Sales

◎ Don't try so hard, the best things come when you least expect them to.

◎ Don't worry about tomorrow, because you do not even know what may happen to you today.

◎ Don't worry about what people think; they don't do it very often.

◎ Everything has beauty, but not everyone sees it.

◎ Happiness comes through doors you didn't even know you left open.

◎ Happiness is enhanced by others but does not depend upon others.

◎ Happy memories never wear out... relive them as often as you want.

◎ He who loses money, loses much. He who loses a friend, loses more. He who loses faith, loses all.

◎ I love your smile. It makes me feel warm on the inside.

◎ If you don't learn to laugh at trouble, you won't have anything to laugh at when you are old.

◎ Jesus is a friend who walks in when the world walks out.

- Just because someone doesn't love you the way you want them to, doesn't mean they don't love you with all they have.
- Just think, you're here not by chance, but by God's choosing to fulfill His special purpose.
- Just thought I'd tell you how special you are to me!
- Keep only cheerful friends. The grouches pull you down.
- Keep your words soft and sweet in case you have to eat them.
- Laughing is good exercise. It's like jogging on the inside.
- Laughter is God's sunshine.
- Let go of what you are and you might become what you could be.
- Let me be your wings
- Life is not about how fast you run, or how high you climb, but how well you bounce.
- Life is not measured by the number of breaths we take, but by the moments that take our breath away.
- Live your life as an exclamation, not an explanation.
- Live your life so that when you die, the preacher will not have to tell lies at your funeral.
- Living well really is the best revenge. Being miserable because of a bad or former relationship just might mean that the other person was right about you.
- Never give up, for that is just the place and time that the tide will turn. - Harriet Beecher Stowe
- Surround yourself with what you love, whether it is family, pets, keepsakes, music, plants, hobbies, whatever. Your home is your refuge.
- Take a walk in the garden of life and enjoy the beauty of it all.
- Take time to laugh for it is the music of the soul.
- The greatest thing in this world is not so much where we are, but in what direction we are moving. - Oliver Holmes
- There's no place I'd rather be than with you!

- The will of God will never take you where the grace of God will not protect you.

- There is no key to happiness. The door is always open.

- There's always a lot to be thankful for if you take time to look for it. For example, I am sitting here thinking how nice it is that wrinkles don't hurt.

- Those who abandon their dreams will discourage yours.

- To achieve the impossible, it is precisely the unthinkable that must be thought. – Tom Robbins

- To handle yourself, use your head. To handle others, use your heart.

- To the world you might be one person, but to one person you might be the world.

- Today when you need a friend to simply hold your hand, close your eyes and feel my presence enfolding you with love. – LaTourelle

- Try not to let your mind wander. It is too small to be out by itself.

- We do not remember days, but moments. Life moves too fast, so enjoy your precious moments.

- We take for granted the things that we should be giving thanks for.

- When life gives you scraps, make quilts.

- You are in my thoughts and in my prayers

- You are richer today if you have laughed, given or forgiven.

- Your friends love you anyway.

A man may die, nations may rise and fall, but an idea lives on.

~ J.F. Kennedy

Go Forth and Prosper

These are the moments...
Be the victor, not the victim.
Smile! It confuses people!
Chocolate solves everything!
Listen to what your heart is saying.
You mean the world to someone, ME!
Some things are only felt with the heart.
A smile is a curve that sets things straight.
Some pursue happiness, others create it.
Imagination is the soul within...
– LaTourelle

Simple pleasures are priceless treasures.

When days are weary and your spirits
are low, remember it is in these
times that God helps us grow!

You must do the thing you think you cannot do. ~ Eleanor Roosevelt

Be who you are and say what you feel
Because those who mind don't matter,
And those who matter don't mind.
– Dr. Seuss

Whenever I think of you, I smile inside. You are beautiful.

You are the strength when the world is weak
You are the light when the world is dark
You are the joy when the sorrow is heavy
You are the love when there is no more
– LaTourelle

*Take a leap of faith and
watch what God can do*

There's no shame to be felt when your efforts
On the top doesn't always place you
As long as you worked your hardest
At the end when each work day was through
Keep your eyes on the goal and you'll reach it
Stay focused as you hold the line
Don't ever give up, you can do it
With diligence, patience and time!
– Jennifer Byerly

*May you find life's simple
beauty in unexpected places.*

Take time to laugh. It is the music of the soul.
Whenever you feel lonely, a special angel drops in for tea.
The soul would have no rainbow, if the eyes had no tears.
No bird soars too high if he soars with his own wings.

*The highest reward for a person's toil
is not what they get for it, but what
they become because of it. ~ Ruskin*

The way to be happy is simple
There's no secret that one must possess
Simply look on the bright side
Always assume for the best

There is gladness in store for the person
Who accepts there are moments with tears
Though trouble may last for awhile
It's happiness that counts through the years

Now the power of joy is quite mighty
And the darkness of anger can break
So choose to be smiling not frowning
But do it for happiness sake!
– Jennifer Byelry

Nothing is beneath you if it is in the direction of your life.
~ Ralph Waldo Emerson

To serve God, to laugh and cry and laugh in spite of it all, to have your priorities in order, to hold a child's heart with love and their hand with encouragement, to learn from the old and give more than you took, to appreciate the touch of the Master's hand, to see the best in others by being the best in yourself, to serve others, to give all you can from your heart not just your bank account, to pray daily, to live contentedly, to keep the faith, to fight the fight and walk the walk, to leave the world a better place than you see it around you, to know that you have made a difference in at least one life, that my friend is honor, integrity, trust, success, the purpose in a life well-lived. – LaTourelle

May God grant you always
A sunbeam to warm you
A moonbeam to guide you
A sheltering angel
So nothing can harm you
May your troubles be few
And your blessings be more
And nothing but happiness
Come through your door

Lives are touched,
Hearts grow
Dreams come true
Because of you.

There are times when your worries
Seem more than you can bear.
Kneel down, close your eyes
Give it to God, He'll answer your prayer.

Success comes in cans;
Failure comes in can'ts.

Let me be your hope when life seems desperate
Let me be your laughter crying through the tears
Let me be the touch that will lift your spirits
Let me be the heart beating strong for you
Let me be your strength when you're feeling weak
Let me be everything to you   – LaTourelle

ENGAGEMENT

- A woman worries about the future until she gets a husband, while a man never worries about the future until he gets a wife.
- A young man in love thinks nothing is good enough for her except himself.
- And I fell in love with you
- Congratulations on this special day
- Diamonds are a girl's best friend and what a gem you have chosen.
- Engaged in Love
- Let the Best Begin Tonight
- Let the Journey Begin
- Love is just a word until you meet that one special person.
- May this be the beginning of a lifetime of love.
- Once Upon a Time
- The best is yet to come
- We've Only Just Begun
- You are my first, my last, my all...
- Young love, sweet love

For better or worse, through thick and thin
You'll be by each other's side
Sharing the laughter and the tears
Through life's uncertain ride.
Nobody knows what the future holds,
We all must wait and see.
But I do know, for the two of you,
The best is yet to be.

Girls will be girls and boys will be boys
Then one day the two hearts will meet
And the rest of the story is oh so sweet!

FaiTh

- 7 days without Prayer makes one weak.
- A little thing is a little thing, but faithfulness in a little thing is a big thing. - Hudson Taylor
- Ask and it shall be given to you; Seek, and you shall find; Knock, and it shall be opened unto you. - Matthew 7:7 KJV
- Each new day brings a new way to praise the Lord.
- Faith... Hope... Love...
- Faith is taking shelter from the storms of life beneath the rainbow of God's love and promises.
- Faith is taking the first step even when you don't see the whole staircase. - Martin Luther King Jr.
- Faith isn't the ability to believe long and far into the misty future. It's simply taking God at His word and taking the next step. - Joni Eareckson Tada
- Faith looks up.
- Faith sees the invisible, believes the incredible and receives the impossible!
- For God so loved the world that He gave His only begotten Son, that whoever believes in Him shall not perish but have eternal life. - John 3:16 NIV
- For the wages of sin is death, but the gift of God is eternal life through Jesus Christ our Lord. - Romans 6:23 NIV
- Give us this day our daily bread
- God Bless America
- God never closes a door without opening a window.
- God placed the rainbow in the sky to remind us that He always keeps His promises
- I AM the Alpha and the Omega, the Beginning and the End. To him who is thirsty I will give to drink without cost from the spring of the water of life. - Revelation 21:6 NIV
- If I keep my eyes on Jesus, I can walk on water.

- If you confess with your mouth, "Jesus as Lord," and believe in your heart that God raised Him from the dead, you shall be saved. - Romans 10:9 NIV
- It takes a little rain to make a rainbow.
- It's me again Lord...
- Jesus answered, "I am the way and the truth and the life. No one comes to the Father except through me." - John 14:6 NIV
- Life is fragile, handle with prayer.
- May the Lord bless you and keep you.
- Now faith is being sure of what we hope for and certain of what we do not see. - Hebrews 11:1 NIV
- Sorrow looks back, Worry looks around, Faith looks up!
- Standing on the promises of God is the best place to be!
- The ability to see and the practice of seeing God and God's world comes through a process of seeking and growing in intimacy with Him. - Dallas Willard
- Trust in the Lord with all your heart.
- When in doubt, read the Bible!

Know your ABC's
Admit that you are a sinner
Believe in the Lord
Confess your sins before Him

Jesus Christ is the same yesterday, today, and forever.
~ Hebrews 13:8 NIV

"You will seek me and find me when you seek me with all your heart. I will be found by you," declares the Lord.
- Jeremiah 29:13-14 NIV

Sometimes we hit a pot hole
As we travel down life's road
The way gets rather bumpy
And we bear a weighty load
Always keep your faith
No matter what you do
Because the path with Jesus
Will be smoother then for you!
– Jennifer Byerly

We may run, walk, stumble, drive,
Or fly, but let us never lose sight of the reason
For the journey, or miss a chance to see
A rainbow on the way.
– Gloria Gaither

Trust Him when doubts seem much stronger.
Trust Him when strength be small,
Trust Him when simply to trust Him
May be the hardest of all.

The thought of You stirs us so deeply
that we cannot be cannot unless we praise
You, because You have made us for Yourself
And our hearts find no peace
Until they rest in You.
– Augustine

God is adequate as our keeper...
Your faith will not fail while God sustains it;
you are not strong enough to fall away
while God is resolved to hold you.
– J. I. Packer

Answering God's Call

God asks that we serve as He calls us
In the place where He wants us to be
He asks that we faithfully follow
What our eyes don't allow us to see
God blesses our lives with our friendships
But his concern is more for the way
We show to the people we're meeting
As we travel life's path every day

God knows that the choices are many
But the answers are simple and sweet
If we stay in His word as we're living
He'll reward us the day that we meet
God knows that the way isn't easy
His son walked this earth as our proof
But He promised us no earthly roses
Just eternal life in His truth!
 – Jennifer Byerly

I believe that I've only one life
To be used in the way that I choose
I believe that it makes not a difference
Whether I win or lose
I believe that one day I will answer
For the choices I made on this earth
And I pray that I'll always choose wisely
And my choices were something of worth!
 – Jennifer Byerly

The adventure of a life time isn't one event.
It's faith in God's goodness which sorrows cannot dent.
It's daily life believing treasures can be found
In just a simple pleasure where love and joy abound.
It's not a destination, we simply don't arrive.
It starts when you can realize, the gift that you're alive!
 – Jennifer Byerly

FaMiLy

- A family alter can alter a family.
- A family is a haven of rest, a sanctuary of peace and most of all a harbor of love.
- A family is a gift that lasts forever.
- A family is a patchwork of love.
- A family is a place for beginning again when we have lost our way.
- Be nice to your kids...they pick your nursing home.
- Big or small, happy families are the best of all.
- Children are natural mimics who act like their parents despite every effort to teach them good manners.
- Family means putting your arms around each other and being there.
- Family memories are held in our hearts forever.
- God bless our family with love
- Grandchildren are loving reminders of what we're really here for.
- Grandchildren don't make a woman feel old: it's being married to a grandfather that bothers her.
- Like branches on a tree, we may grow in different directions, yet our roots remain as one.
- Other things may change us, but we start and end with family.
- Some family trees bear enormous crops of nuts.
- Some of the happiest moments in life are those we share with my family.
- What we need are more family trees that will produce more lumber and fewer nuts.
- Families—the one true home, no matter where you live.

FAREWELL

- As you go out on your new job, your new adventure, don't forget the little people who held your hand along the way.

- Blessings on your new adventure.

- Don't be dismayed by goodbyes. A farewell is necessary before you can meet again. And meeting again, after moments or lifetimes, is certain for those who are friends. - Richard Bach

- Every farewell combines loss & new freedom. - Mason Cooley

- Farewell, farewell, you old rhinoceros, I'll stare at something less prepoceros. - Ogden Nash

- Goodbye is so hard to say... How I wish you could stay.

- Goodbye. You will be missed more than you know.

- I do not wish for you to walk out the door and away from me forever more.

- I have a long journey to take, and must bid the company farewell. - Walter Raleigh

- May the Lord watch over you and keep you always.

- There are no goodbyes among friends.

- Today is a day I knew we would have to come to... It seems it came so quickly... - CC Milam

- Until our paths cross again, Peace to you.

- Wherever you go, no matter what the weather, always bring your sunshine. - Anthony J. D'Angelo

Tis always sad when friends must part
the times they hold so dear...
So let this path come round again
and bring us ever near!
~ Irish Blessing

May the road rise to meet you,
May the wind be always at your back,
May the sunshine warm upon your face,
The rains fall soft upon your fields and,
Until we meet again,
May God hold you in the palm of His hand.
– Irish Blessing

May God grant you always
A sunbeam to warm you
A moonbeam to charm you
A sheltering angel so nothing can harm you
Laughter to cheer you
Faithful friends near you
And whenever you pray
Heaven to hear you.
– Irish Blessing

Even though I am leaving
I'll never leave your side
I'll be there for you
Even through your bumpiest rides
When you feel like you can't cope anymore
That's where I'll come in
I'll try my best to make you feel loved
So please keep up your chin
Things will get tough
And we'll shed some tears
We'll feel pain and anger
But our future is clear.
Never think that no one cares
Because I definitely do
Distance can't keep us apart
especially from me loving you.
I hope our friendship never dies.
I'll miss you so very much
You are definitely a beautiful friend
And I know we'll never lose touch.

FaTheR's Day

- # 1 Dad
- A father carries pictures where his money used to be.
- A father is compassion, strength, wisdom and love!
- A truly rich man is one whose children run into his arms when his hands are empty.
- Any man can be a father. It takes someone special to be a dad.
- Daddy come play ball with me, let's shoot or toss or catch the ball, for just being with you, Daddy is the most fun of all!
- Daddy you're the best!
- Fatherhood is pretending the present you love most is soap-on-a-rope. - Bill Cosby
- Fathers are a work of heart.
- Have you noticed that it cost more to amuse your children now than your college education?
- He's my Dad!
- Hop on Pop
- My Daddy hung the moon
- My heart belongs to Daddy
- No one can fill your shoes
- Of all the gifts I've ever received, the gift I cherish most is YOU. Happy Father's Day - LaTourelle
- Oh how I love Daddy!
- Our Dad has a heart of gold.

When I was a boy of fourteen, my father was so ignorant I could hardly stand to have the old man around. But when I got to be twenty-one, I was astonished at how much he had learned in seven years.

— Mark Twain

DAD:
Someone who hopes his son
will turn out just like him,
and who is afraid his daughters
will meet someone who did.

A Father's Day Prayer for You

Dear Lord, please watch over my father
For he is very special to me.
Bless each day in all that he does.
And let him the wonders of you see,
And bring him home safely, for him I miss,
Then, I can give him a big hug and kiss.

Dad,

I love you with a special love that
deepens throughout the years.
You are the best! Have a great day!

Your faith in God and how you live your life makes it so
easy to place my trust in our Heavenly Father.
Happy Father's Day

Dad dreams, he plans, he struggles
That we might have the best,
His sacrifice is quiet,
His life is love expressed.

The best inheritance a father can leave his children is
a good example. Thank you dad for leading our family and
for loving mom. My life is blessed with you as my father.
Happy Father's Day

Thank you for being there
Through the years to listen,
To cheer me on, to support me,
To love me...
Happy Father's Day

Thanks
For giving me the
Best things in life—
Your time, your care, your love.
Happy Father's Day

You're so great
I couldn't have picked
A better dad if I tried.
Happy Dad's Day
I want to share the
Best in me with others
Because it came
From you.

Thank you for unconditional love and
Encouragement everyday of my life.
You are the bestest Father that
A child could ever hope for!
Happy Dad's Day

Dad's Tools

Dependability, Faith in God,
Dedication, Stability,
Fairness, Pride.
Love

FOURTh OF JULY

America

Oh the land of lands, my Fatherland,
The beautiful, the free,
All lands and shores to freedom dear,
Are ever dear to thee;
All sons of freedom hail thy name
And wait thy word of might,
While round the world the list are joined
For liberty and light.

United we stand,
Forever in freedom it waves...
God Bless America

Our flag is red, white and blue,
but America is a rainbow
Red and yellow, black and white
we are precious in His sight.

God Bless America
The red, white and blue
May her colors wave proudly
Over each one of you!
– Jennifer Byerly

Your flag and my flag
The red, white and blue
We pledge to our country
Hearts that are true.
– Jennifer Byerly

American Creed:

Patriotism which leaps over the fence of party prejudice. Religion which jumps over the wall of intolerance. Brotherhood which climbs over the mountain of national separations. We must be willing to pay a price for freedom, for no price that is ever asked for it is half the cost of doing without it.

FRIENDS

- A friend in need is a friend indeed. - Latin Proverb
- A friend is one who joyfully sings with you when you are on a mountaintop, and silently walks beside you through the valley. - William A. Ward
- A friend understands what you are trying to say. Even when your thoughts aren't fitting into words. - Ann D. Parrish
- A good friend is cheaper than therapy.
- A loyal friend laughs at your jokes when they're not so good, and sympathizes with your problems when they're not so bad. - Arnold H. Glasgow
- A true friend is someone who reaches for your hand and touches your heart.
- Alone we can do so little; together we can do so much. - Helen Keller
- And in the sweetness of friendship let there be laughter, and sharing of pleasures.
- Books and friends should be few but good.
- For without words, in friendship, all thoughts, all desires, all expectations are born and shared, with joy that is unclaimed.
- Friends have all things in common. - Plato
- Friendship is always a sweet responsibility, never an opportunity. - Kahil Gibran
- Friendship is love with wings.
- Friendship is the only thing in the world concerning the usefulness of which all mankind are agreed. - Cicero
- Friendship that flows from the heart cannot be frozen by adversity, as the water that flows from the spring cannot congeal in winter. - James Fenimore Cooper
- Friendship without self interest is one of the rare and beautiful things in life. - James Francis Byrnes

- Grief can take care of itself, but to get the full value of joy you must have somebody to divide it with. – Mark Twain

- I never came to you, my friend, and went away without some new enrichment of the heart; more faith and less of doubt. – Grace Cowell

- I no doubt deserved my enemies, but I don't believe I deserved my friends. – Walt Whitman

- I see you when I look in the mirror of friendship.

- I will speak ill of no man, and speak all the good I know of everybody. – Benjamin Franklin

- It is a sweet thing, friendship, a dear balm, a happy and auspicious bird of calm... – Shelly

- Life is partly what we make it, and partly what is made by the friends whom we choose. – Tehyi Hsieh

- Love is blind–friendship closes its eyes.

- Many people will walk in and out of your life, but only true friends will leave footprints in your heart.

- May our friendship never stop blooming. – CC Milam

- My love doth hold you close at heart, in friendship dear right from the start. – LaTourelle

- No soul is desolate as long as there is a human being for whom it can feel trust and reverence. – George Eliot

- One can never speak enough of the virtues, the dangers, the power of shared laughter. – Francoise Sagan

- Real friends are those who, when you feel you've made a fool of yourself, don't feel you've done a permanent job.

- Some people go to priests; others to poetry; I to my friends. – Virginia Woolf

- Stay is a charming word in a friend's vocabulary. – Louisa May Alcott

- The best mirror is an old friend. – George Herbert

- The best way to keep your friends is not to give them away. – Wilson Mizner

- The friend is the man who knows all about you, and still likes you. - Elbert Hubbard
- The friendship that can cease has never been real. - Saint Jerome
- The happiest moments my heart knows are those in which it is pouring forth its affections to a few esteemed characters. - Thomas Jefferson
- The making of friends, who are real friends, is the best token we have of a man's success in life. - Edward Everett Hale
- The only thing to do is to hug one's friends tight and do one's job. - Edith Wharton
- Think where man's glory most begins and ends, and say my glory was I had such friends. - William Yeats
- This communicating of a man's self to his friend works two contrary effects; for it redoubled joy, and cutteth griefs in half. - Francis Bacon
- Thus nature has no love for solitude, and always leans, as it were, on some support; and the sweetest support is found in the most intimate friendship. - Cicero
- To have a friend, be a friend.
- Too late we learn, a man must hold his friend Un-judged, accepted, trusted to the end. - John Boyle O'Reilly
- True friendship is what I found in you!
- What is a friend? A single soul in two bodies. - Aristotle
- What sunshine is to flowers, smiles are to humanity. They are but trifles, to be sure, but scattered along life's pathway, the good they do is inconceivable.
- When I think of a friend, I think of Jesus. Be a friend as He was a friend—showing unconditional love and kindness.
- Without friends no one would choose to live, though he had all other goods. - Aristotle
- Your gentleness made you my friend. Your compassion made you my confidant and your strength in adversity made you my hero.

Every act of kindness moves to a larger one till friendships bloom to show what little deeds have done. - June Masters Bacher

I find friendship to be like wine, raw when new, ripened with age, the true old man's milk and restorative cordial.
 - Thomas Jefferson

Friendship is unnecessary, like philosophy, like art... It has no survival value; rather it is one of those things that give value to survival. - C.S. Lewis

The best kind of friend is the one you could sit on a porch with, never saying a word, and walk away feeling like that was the best conversation you've had.

I do not wish to treat friendships daintily, but with the roughest courage. When they are real, they are not glass threads or frost-work, but the solidest thing we know.
 - Ralph Waldo Emerson

The most I can do for my friend is simply to be his friend. I have no wealth to bestow on him. If he knows that I am happy in loving him, he will want no other reward. Is not friendship divine in this? - Henry David Thoreau

In everyone's life, at some time, our inner fire goes out. It is then burst into flame by an encounter with another human being. We should all be thankful for those people who rekindle the inner spirit. - Albert Schweitzer

We are not enemies, but friends. We must not be enemies. Though passion may have strained, it must not break our bonds of affection. The mystic cords of memory will swell when again touched as surely they will be by the better angels of our nature. - Abraham Lincoln

Large pink petal roses with long green stems,
White daisy flowers all neat and trimmed.
A gift of love... sent from a friend...
– GG Milam

Whether near or far apart
Your friendship brews within my heart
Soothing angst deep in my soul
It fills my cup to overflow!
– Jennifer Byerly

I know our lives get busy
We're always on the go
But I'd so enjoy a visit
At anytime you know
I really love your company
And having you around!
Whenever I spend time with you
An endless joy abounds!
– Jennifer Byerly

*No man is useless
while he has a friend*

There are good ships, wood ships
And ships that sail the sea
But the best ships are friendships,
and may we always be...

Have you ever seen a sunset grand, been caressed by
a baby's hand, gleaned the wisdom from an old man's
face, experienced the freedom of immeasurable grace?
Then you, my friend, are blessed so much. Thanks to the love
of your Master's touch. So know that today and forever more
His awesome power will carry you far. Don't welcome worry as
an old friend. Give it up daily, for joy without end.   – LaTourelle

The bird a nest,
The spider a web,
Man friendship.
– William Blake

I wish for you a sunny day
with skies so blue
and time to pray
I wish for you a song-filled heart
a peace so delightful
with love from the start
– LaTourelle

Tweedle-dee and tweedle-dum
Love to play with hugs and fun
Laughter and smiles the whole day through
Oh what a joy when shared by two
– LaTourelle

Please don't be a stranger
And know that you are free
To join me for a visit
And have share some laughs with me!
– Jennifer Byerly

When true friends meet in adverse hour:
'Tis like a sunbeam through a shower.
A watery way an instant seen,
The darkly closing clouds between.
– Sir Walter Scott

By these words may you always know
That my love is with you wherever you go
~ LaTourelle

I wish for you a sunrise
So spectacular to view
I wish for you a sunset
As magnificent as you
– LaTourelle

Oh what a beautiful face
Filled with such beauty and grace
Your smile is divine
Your love so sublime
Thank you for giving to me
All that I ever did need
– LaTourelle

I Love you dearly and am so
Blessed to call you friend!
~ LaTourelle

When you look inside this present
There's a gift that's meant to be
A hug across the miles
Full of love from me
– Jennifer Byerly

It's amazingly clear
There's nothing so dear
As a friend by your side
Along for the ride

When one is helping another both are strong
Thank you for giving me strength
And a friendship I cherish
I Love You

When Prayers Go Up...
Blessings Come Down

When I count my many blessings
It isn't hard to see
The greatest gift I have
Is the love you have for me
– LaTourelle

Knowing that someone cares
and holds us close in their prayers
Knowing that we're understood
Makes everyday living feel wonderfully good
– LaTourelle

I'm so glad I have a friend like you
To lean on when I'm feeling blue
To pick me up and help me stand
To reach out and lend a hand
You're there for me through and through
I'm so glad I have a friend like you!
In Honor Linda LaTourelle
by GG Milam April 24, 2005

Biblical Friendship Quotes

◉ A friend loves at all times. – Proverbs 17:17 NIV

◉ A man of many companions may come to ruin, but there is a friend who sticks closer than a brother. – Proverbs 18:24 NIV

◉ Dear friends, let us love one another, for love comes from God. – I John 4:7 NIV

◉ Faithful are the wounds of a friend; but the kisses of an enemy are deceitful. – Proverbs 27:6 KJV

◉ Greater love hath no man than this' that a man lay down his life for his friends. – John 15:13 KJV

Girl-Friends

Everyone everywhere
The whole world through
Needs a girlfriend
Just like you!
Others are important
You know we love them, too
Yet, there are special times
When only a girlfriend will do!

Diva Sisters

Friends are the rainbow in the morning
dewdrop and the fragrance in the evening breeze
Lemonade on a hot summer day
tea in the afternoon or hot chocolate
on a wintry night; some things
just go better with a friend

Thanks for being there when
everyone else walked out

It's wonderful to have a friend
One on whom you can depend
To chat and giggle with schoolgirl glee,
To sit and sip a cup of tea -La Tourelle

Girlfriends are Forever Friends

Intimacies between women often go backwards,
Beginning in revelations and ending in small talk.
– Elizabeth Bowen

Best friends are like diamonds,
precious and rare.

Old Friends

Wandering back through the rivers of time
As special memories flood my mind
People and places that once meant so much
Now we rarely even keep in touch
We went to your house you came to our home
So long ago, before the children were grown
We went out for dinner, even danced a few
Oh, the secrets we shared between me and you
I recently walked through the old neighborhood
The houses now seemed just stucco and wood
New families now making their own memories
Raising their children and sowing their seeds
Although we have parted and gone our own ways
I sometimes journey back to those familiar days
To you my friends, I'll lift my glass
As long as there's memories, friendships will last!
– Barbara K. Cox

*I count myself in nothing else so happy as in
a soul remembering my good friends.
~ William Shakespeare*

There is magic in the memory of schoolboy friendships: it softens the heart, and even affects the nervous system of those who have no heart. – Benjamin Disraeli

*The death of a friend is equivalent to
the loss of a limb. ~ German Proverb*

With every friend I love who has been taken into the brown bosom of the earth a part of me has been buried there; but their contribution to my being of happiness, strength and understanding remains to sustain me in an altered world. – Helen Keller

GARDENERS

- A beautiful garden is your reward for doing God's yard work.
- A garden is a friend you can visit any time.
- All things grow with love.
- Bless my flowers & my weeds. Bless my birdies & bees.
- Bloom where you are planted.
- Families are all grown in the same garden.
- Flowers of true friendship never fade.
- Friends are flowers in the garden of life.
- Friends are the flowers of heaven.
- Hearts that love are always in bloom.
- If friends were flowers, I'd pick you.
- My world without you for a friend would be like a garden full of weeds.
- One is never nearer to God's heart than in a garden.
- Pleasant words are as a honeycomb, sweet to the soul, and health to the bones. - Proverbs 16:24 NIV
- Sun shines, birds sing, garden angels flowers bring...
- The song of a robin is an angels voice in the garden.
- There is peace in the garden and His beauty along the path.
- Time began in a Garden
- When you kneel in your garden, take time to pray.
- Wildflowers are like friends-they always come back.
- Your love is the nurturing touch.
- Your seeds of love have changed my life. Thanks!

For lo, the winter is past, the rain is over and gone: The flowers appear on the earth: the time of the singing of birds is come, and the voice of the turtle is heard in our land. - Song of Solomon 2:11-12 KJV

For the Garden of Your Daily Living…

PLANT THREE ROWS OF PEAS:
1. Peace of mind
2. Peace of heart
3. Peace of Soul

PLANT FOUR ROWS OF SQUASH:
1. Squash gossip
2. Squash indifference
3. Squash grumbling
4. Squash selfishness

PLANT FOUR ROWS OF LETTUCE:
1. Lettuce be faithful
2. Lettuce be kind
3. Lettuce be patient
4. Lettuce really love one another

NO GARDEN IS WITHOUT TURNIPS:
1. Turnip for meetings
2. Turnip for service
3. Turnip to help one another

TO CONCLUDE OUR GARDEN WE MUST HAVE THYME:
1. Thyme for each other
2. Thyme for family
3. Thyme for friends

Water freely with patience and cultivate with love.
There is much fruit in your garden
because you reap what you sow.

Come to the garden alone, while the dew is still on the roses…

Gardening Rule:
When weeding, the best way to make sure you are removing
a weed and not a valuable plant is to pull on it. If it comes out
of the ground easily, it is a valuable plant.

May all your days be glowing
With sunny moments bright
May your joy be blossoming
Morning, noon and night!
– Jennifer Byerly

Grow where you are planted

Don't look for greener fields
God's word will be your sunlight
His promise is your shield
His love will be the soil
To sink your roots within
So you can bear a rich crop
Of fruit from deep within
– Jennifer Byerly

I meant to do my work today,
But a brown bird sang in the apple tree,
And a butterfly flitted across the field,
And all the flowers were calling me.

Like a Rose

Your scent is that of many flowers
You stand so tall against the others
Your beauty is surely perfection
Although it seems to need a lot of protection
Your pure silk texture flows in the wind
You seem so brittle, so unkind
The love I have for you can never die
Your thorns hurt really bad
I'll try to learn not to make you sad
Your roots run deep and true
Your stem so reliable for much needed support
You shine above the rest in my little cottage garden
You my love are my favorite flower!
– Kerry Higgins

GET WELL

- ◉ Being in the hospital is a downer but look on the bright side you get breakfast in bed! Cheery Day!
- ◉ Come to me, all ye that labour and are heavy laden, and I will give you rest. - Matthew 1128 KJV
- ◉ Get Well Soon. Sorry you're not feeling your best. Sure hope you're better soon! Best Wishes
- ◉ Hospital food is encouragement for a quick recovery.
- ◉ It won't be long before you're all better and back to being your same old self again–enjoy this rest while it lasts!
- ◉ May the God of all comfort bring you peace and healing.
- ◉ May the Lord be with you and you feel His healing touch.
- ◉ Our warmest thoughts and prayers are with you. Wishing you a speedy recovery.
- ◉ Sending happy thoughts to brighten your day.
- ◉ Sending hugs and kisses and really big get well wishes.
- ◉ Sending a note your way to let you know that someone cares and is keeping you in their prayers.
- ◉ The colder the X-ray table, the more of your body is required on it. Hope you're home soon!
- ◉ The really happy man is the one who can enjoy the scenery when he has to take a detour. Sorry about your accident.
- ◉ Thinking of you. May you feel better soon.
- ◉ Wishing you a speedy recovery and happy days!

Here's to feelin' better
Here's to getting' well
Here's to "have no worries"
'Cause we'll bring in your mail
And Here's to waterin' flowers
And walking your dog too
Here's to all the things you need
'Cause we'll be there for you!
– Jennifer Byerly

With the warmest of wishes
This just comes to say
Hope that you're feeling
Much better today

So you're sick
Look on the bright side
Now you finally
Have a reason to
Whine and complain!
Get Well Soon

Let there be sunshine
To chase the clouds away
Kind thoughts to cheer you
And brighten your day

Good wishes are sent with these flowers
In hopes that you'll always see
Blue sky and cheerful moments
Whatever the weather may be
– Jennifer Byerly

A Prayer for Your Recovery
Was sent Heavenward today
I trusted God to guide me
In just how I ought to pray.
So I am trusting that He heard me
And you will soon be feeling fine
And we will rejoice together
Dearest friend of mine!
– Thena Smith

He who has health has hope, but he who
has hope has everything

❧

Here's a little message
Especially for you
We hope you're soon back on your feet
And feeling better too!
– Jennifer Byerly

I wish for you a sunny day
with skies so blue and time to pray.
I wish for you a song-filled heart,
a peace so delightful
with love from the start.

You are in my Thoughts

Sometimes our lives bring things
that we don't understand
And it is difficult to see
just where was the Master's hand

But God will work all things out
if we just give him the chance to do
The things He knows are the best
and then He will see us through
– Thena Smith

Hope is the thing with feathers
That perches in the soul
And sings the tune without the words
And never stops–at all
And sweetest–in the Gale–is heard
And sore must be the storm
That could abash the little Bird
That keeps so many warm
I've heard it in the chilliest land
And on the strangest Sea
Yet, never, in Extremity
It asked a crumb–of Me
– Emily Dickinson

GOD IS LOVE

- And we know that all things work together for good for them that love God. - Romans 8:28 KJV

- For I am convinced that neither death nor life, ...Nor things present, nor things to come, ...shall be able to separate us from the love of God. - Romans 8:37-39 NIV

- God is the friend of silence. Trees, flowers, grass grow in silence. See the stars, moon, and sun how they move in silence. - Mother Teresa

- God loves each of us as if there were only one of us. - Augustine

- Healed by Your love, corruption and decay are turned, and whole, we greet the light of day. - Madeleine L'Engle

- How great is the love the Father has lavished on us, that we should be called children of God! And that is what we are! - 1 John 3:1 NIV

- If God had a refrigerator, your picture would be on it!

- Jesus accepts you the way you are, but loves you too much to leave you that way. - Lee Venden

- Jesus said, "These things I have spoken unto you, that in Me ye might have peace. In the world ye shall have tribulation: but be of good cheer; I have overcome the world." - John 16:33 KJV

- Love the Lord your God with all your heart and with all your soul and with all your mind. - Matthew 22:37 NIV

- Now unto Him that is able to do exceeding abundantly above all that we ask or think! - Ephesians 3:20 KJV

- The Lord is gracious, and full of compassion; slow to anger, and of great mercy. - Psalm 145:8 KJV

- The secret of the mystery is: God is always greater. No matter how great we think Him to be, His love is always greater. - Bennan Manning

- The steadfast love of the Lord never ends. His mercies are new every morning. Great is Thy faithfulness. - Lamentations 3:22-23 KJV

The wonder of living is held within the
beauty of silence, the glory of sunlight...
The sweetness of fresh spring air,
the quiet strength of earth,
and the love that lies at the
very root of all things.

The work of creating is an act of love.
The God who flung from His fingertips this
universe filled with galaxies and stars,
penguins and puffins, gulls and gannets...
peaches and pears, and a world full of children
made in His own image, is the God who
loves with magnificent monotony.
– Brennan Manning

Where can I go from your Spirit?
Where can I flee from your presence?
If I go up to the heavens, you are there;
If I make my bed in the depths, you are there.
If I rise on the wings of the dawn,
If I settle on the far side of the sea,
Even there your hand will guide me,
Your right hand will hold me fast.
– Psalm 139: 7-10 NIV

From the tiny birds of the air and from the
fragile lilies of the field we learn the same truth,
which is so important for those who desire a
life of simple faith: God takes care of His own.
He knows our needs. He anticipates our crises...
He stands ready to come to our rescue.
And at just the right moment He steps in and
proves Himself as our faithful heavenly Father.
– Charles R. Swindoll

The Fabric of Your Life

The fabric of your life is what
Makes you what you are.
Some people leave a mark
Some leave a scar.
Parents who love you
Day by day and guide
Your steps along the way.
Grandparents who love you for who you are,
Whether they live near or very far.
With brothers and sisters, you share so much.
Love and arguments are part of growing up.
Uncles and aunts, neighbors and friends,
Preachers and teachers, employers, too,
All have a part in making you, "you."
More important than all of these,
Is the one on who you can call whenever you please,
Whether standing tall or down on your knees.
Out on your own, away from home,
He's closer than Mom on the phone.
His plans have been in place
Before anyone looked upon your face.
Let God guide you through each day.
He will weave a beautiful tapestry
Out of the fabrics of your life
And that tapestry is YOU!
– Linda Zimmerman

A Love So True

God made the mountains majesty
And oceans bold and restless
He lifted up His hands with light
And painted landscapes breathless
But in a whisper soft and low
He gave to us a child aglow
To come and live with us today
Forever thankful we shall pray
His love for us is ever grand
And so we praise Him as we stand
For giving us His endless grace
To honor holy that precious face
Thank you Lord for all you do
But most of all for Love so true
– Linda LaTourelle

God expresses beauty
In a very special way
By giving each a special place
Inside life's sweet bouquet
– Jennifer Byerly

Green grass and baby blue sky,
The sounds of a baby's cry,
The rose how it seems so sweet,
Like the day we will sit at the Lord's feet.
– August Jones

His love can move the mountains
His love can calm the sea
His love is always reaching out
To encircle you and me!
– Thena Smith

GRADUATION

- ◉ A Darling with a Diploma
- ◉ All I need to know I learned in Kindergarten.
- ◉ Awesome Grad!
- ◉ Be All You Can Be
- ◉ Be nice to the nerds and geeks in high school... You'll be working for them in the future.
- ◉ Beautiful Tomorrows
- ◉ Brainiac with Papers to Prove it!
- ◉ By the skin of my teeth
- ◉ Congratulations Graduate!
- ◉ Dreams are as real as we believe them to be. Follow your heart wherever it leads you. - Flavia
- ◉ Education Celebration
- ◉ Graduate life—it's not just a job, it's an indenture.
- ◉ Hat's Off to You!
- ◉ I is a college student.
- ◉ It is indeed ironic that we spend our school days yearning to graduate and our remaining days waxing nostalgic about our school day. - Isabel Waxman
- ◉ Look out world! Here I come!
- ◉ Measure wealth not by the things you have, but by the things you have for which you would not take money.
- ◉ Never be afraid to try something new. Remember that a lone amateur built the Ark. A large group of professionals built the Titanic.
- ◉ No more summer vacation.
- ◉ Now Willing to Consider C.E.O. Position
- ◉ School's out, memories pass. Don't ever doubt, our friendship will last.

◉ The fireworks begin today. Each diploma is a lighted match, and you are its fuse. - Ed Koch

◉ The tassel is worth the hassle

◉ There is no need to reach high for the stars. They are already within you—just reach deep into yourself.

◉ This is the first day of the rest of your life.

◉ Where your talents and the needs of the world cross lies your calling. - Aristotle

◉ You cannot help but learn more as you take the world into your hands. Take it up reverently, for it is an old piece of clay, with millions of thumbprints on it. - John Updike

◉ Your future is an unwritten symphony—just awaiting your creative daring and unique talent to make it a Masterpiece.

Twenty years from now you will be more
disappointed by the things you didn't do than by
the ones you did do. So throw off the bowlines.
Sail away from the safe harbor. Catch the trade
winds in your sails. Explore. Dream. Discover.
- Mark Twain

For I know the plans I have for you, declares the Lord,
plans to prosper you and not to harm you, plans to
give you hope and a future. - Jeremiah 29:11 NIV

Trust in the LORD with all your heart and lean not on your own
understanding; in all your ways acknowledge Him, and
He will make your paths straight. - Proverbs 3:5-6 NIV

Today is a day you have worked hard for and have been waiting.
Today is a day of accomplishments and pride;
Pride in reaching your goals and living your dream come true.
May you continue to go forward into the future and
receive the desires of your heart.

Young woman, my daughter,
My joy and my heart,
You've reached the end
Only to find a new start!
The world sees the young woman
With her charm and her smile,
But behind the woman,
I will always see the child.

Congratulations Graduate

You served your time
And learned quite well
Now finally the day is here
When all that love you, oh so dear,
Can raise their hands and bid you cheer!!
Enjoy this day and all it means
For your journey now begins
So throw your cap into the air
And be proud of how far you've come
Happy Graduation Day!

Your World Is Different

Your world is different today
Than it was yesterday.
And each special moment is worth recording
From the simplest routine day
To the best and most rewarding.
In this book are photos of fun-filled times
With family and friends galore
And before this book is completed
And sits on a shelf...
There will be many, many more.
Enjoy your days as each one comes
And enjoy the memories recorded herein.
For with this album you hold in your hands
You can enjoy them again and again!
– Thena Smith

On Your Kindergarten Graduation

Today is a first of many special days to come—
With your cap and gown you will walk
Across the stage—out of kindergarten
into your future school years.
We are so proud of you today
as we see our little girl—
a young lady before us.
We love you and remember,
God's not finished with you yet!
– GG Milam

Happy Kindergarten Graduation Day!

You are my Katie Bug Ladybug
Always here to give me a hug.
I love you and your kisses so sweet
And to tickle your belly and wiggly feet.
You are the sunshine in each new day,
And I love you dear, in everyway.
Happy Kindergarten Graduation
– GG Milam

High School Graduation is a reflection of memories.
Memories of getting an education,
Relationships with classmates,
School pride and spirit.
Congratulations on this special day!
May you always cherish your youth.

As You Graduate from College

Congratulations,
On all of your accomplishments!
May you look back to this one special day
When at last your dreams of being a
college graduate came true.
Best Wishes on a Happy Future

GRANDPARENT'S DAY

- A Grandma fills the world with love.
- A Grandpa is a special friend.
- Bounce me one more time, please.
- CAUTION: Grandparents at play.
- Grandma: a child with a checkbook and a driver's license.
- Grandma's cookies make the rainy days sunny.
- Grandmas are earth angels.
- Grandmas are just antique little girls.
- Grandma's my name, spoiling's my game.
- Grandpa is my best friend (Grandma.)
- Grandpa–My Hero
- Granny and Papa, love you with all the world.
- My heart belongs to Grandpa (Grandma.)
- Nanny's Nest is Best but Papa Rules the Roost
- Nobody does it better, only my Grandma.
- One old crow and a cute little chick live here.
- Thanks for spoiling me rotten and not telling mom.
- There's no place like home except at Grandma's.
- There's no place like my Nannie and Papa's.
- They don't stop and see. I'm glad that God made Grandpa, unrushed, and young like me.
- Time with Grandpa is a lesson in his-story!
- When Mom says no...call 1-800-Grandma.
- When you need a hug call 1-800-Grandpa.
- You're–Great, Wise and so Fun I guess that's why you're called "Grand"pa.

*My grandma is great at sewing
the family together with love.*

Grandma, it's important you know
How special you are to me
There is no one quite as precious
Thank you for loving me so

Dearest Grandma,
    When I say my prayers at night
I thank the Lord for love so right
Grandma you fill my life with fun
In all the world your the only one

Grandpa,
Can you guess
What I want to be
When I grow up?
As fun and smart as you!
Happy Grandfathers' Day

Happiest Grandpa's Day
It's so great to have a Grandpa
who loves to play and have fun,
but the reason that I love you
is just because you're the one!
Happy Grandfather's Day, Grandpa

Walking with Grandpa
I like to walk with Grandpa,
His steps are short like mine.
He doesn't say "Now Hurry Up,"
He always takes his time.
I like to walk with Grandpa,
His eyes see things like mine do-
Wee pebbles bright, a funny cloud,
Half hidden drops of dew.
Most people have to hurry,

HALLOWEEN

- Carving out memories, one pumpkin at a time. - LaTourelle
- Costumes and Pumpkins and Candy Corn, Oh My!
- Our pumpkin smiles at us upon the window sill. We're stuffed with lots of candy and now feel very ill. - LaTourelle
- Trick or Treat! Smell my feet. Give me something good to eat!
- You look cute as can be! Is that you under there I see??

Pumpkin Patch
Going to the pumpkin patch
Is so much fun.
There are so many pumpkins
To choose from
We'll look and look
Until we find the right one
Going to the pumpkin patch
Is so much fun!
- Linda Zimmerman

I love your cute pumpkin smile,
And your little pumpkin frame
Your teeny tiny pumpkin toes
And your sweet pumpkin name!
Yes, you're my favorite pumpkin
The cutest I could ever hope to see
And I will tell everyone that I meet
That the cutest pumpkin belongs to me!
- Thena Smith

You are my favorite pumpkin!
You are the cutest in the patch.
I love your little pumpkin nose
And pumpkin eyes that match!
~ Thena Smith

Hanukkah

- A wish for you at Hanukkah
- As you light each candle, may your heart feel love.
- Dreidle, Dreidle, Dreidle
- Especially for you at Chanukah
- Festival of Lights
- Happy Hanukkah to you
- Hold onto tradition–Happy Hanukkah.
- Holy Lights
- Lighting the Menorah
- One Candle More
- Sending you Hanukkah prayers.
- Shalom
- We kindle these lights.
- Wishing you a very Happy Chanukah.
- With Warmest Chanukah Wishes.

Today we light the Chanukah menorah
With eight branches to glow so bright
And for eight days we do this
Adding one new candle each night

We will spin the Dreidle
Our top that is such fun
We will have good things to eat
And enjoy each and every one.

Latkes and sufganiyot
Are among our special treats
But Chanukah is a special celebration
Of much more than just good eats
- Thena Smith

You are a Blessing

Let's light the menorah
For the Festival of Lights,
One candle every evening
For eight great, joyous nights

We have a blessing for the lights
and for the Yom Tov, too,
But of all the blessings in my life...
The greatest one is you.

You're someone who is very
dear and very special, too...
And lots of love comes with this
wish at Chanukah for you!

Chanukah is a time of miracles,
so it seems the perfect time
to let you know how thankful I am
for the miracle of having you in my life...

Chanukah is a time of light and joy—
and so it is the perfect time to think of you,
for bringing blessings and laughter to my life.
Happy Chanukah

You Are Very Special to Me,

There is a light that shines from within you
Bringing warmth and light to
Those around that you touch—
You do this in your own special way...
Thank you for being a very special part of my life.
Happy Hanukkah

HOUSE AND HOME

◎ A hundred men may make an encampment, but it takes a woman to make a home. – Chinese Proverb

◎ A man's home may be his castle, but this one does not come with servants.

◎ A messy kitchen is a happy kitchen... and this kitchen is delirious.

◎ A mother's love is the heart of the home

◎ A nest isn't empty until all their stuff is out of the attic.

◎ Bless this house

◎ Bless this mess

◎ But if serving the LORD seems undesirable to you, then choose for yourselves this day whom you will serve, whether the gods your forefathers served beyond the River, or the gods of the Amorites, in whose land you are living. But as for me and my household, we will serve the LORD. – Joshua 24:15 NIV

◎ Cabin Sweet Cabin

◎ Christ is the Head of this house, The unseen Guest at every meal, the silent Listener to every conversation.

◎ Cleaning house while children are growing is like shoveling snow while it's still snowing.

◎ Condo Sweet Condo

◎ Do not store up for yourselves treasures on earth... But store up for yourselves treasures in heaven... For where your treasure is, there will your heart be also. – Matthew 6:19-21 NIV

◎ Dull women have immaculate homes.

◎ Dust is a country accent.

◎ Enter with a happy heart, leave with a full belly.

◎ Family ties are precious threads, no matter where we roam... They draw us close to those we love, and pull our hearts toward home.

- He is the happiest, be he king or peasant, who finds peace in his home. - Johann Wolfgang von Goethe
- Help keep the kitchen clean—eat out.
- Home interprets heaven. Home is heaven for beginners. - Charles H. Parkhurst
- Home is not where you live, but where they understand you. - Christian Morgenstern
- Home is the most popular, and will be the most enduring of all earthly establishments. - Channing Pollock
- Home is the place where we grumble the most, but are often treated the best.
- Home is the place where, when you have to go there, They have to take you in. - Robert Frost
- Home is where the heart is.
- Home is where the Lord sends us.
- Home is where you can say anything you like, because nobody listens to you anyway.
- Home is where your family is.
- Home is where you hang your heart.
- Home is where you make your nest.
- Home is where your honey is.
- Home is where...they have to let you in!
- Home, the spot of earth supremely blest, A dearer, sweeter spot than all the rest. - Robert Montgomery
- Housework can kill you if done right. - Erma Bombeck
- It's always darkest before dawn. So if you're going to steal your neighbor's newspaper, that's the time to do it.
- Little angels up above: Bless our home with lots of love.
- My house was clean yesterday... Sorry you missed it.
- Never keep up with the Joneses. Drag them down to your level. - Quentin Crisp
- Never far from home will I ever roam. - CC Milam

- So this isn't Home Sweet Home... Adjust!
- The Bible tells us to love our neighbors, and also to love our enemies, probably because they are generally the same people.
- The easiest way to find something lost around the house is to buy a replacement.
- The father is the head of the house and the mother is the heart of the house.
- There's no place like home. - Dorothy
- This home protected by a coat of dust.
- We need not power or splendor, wide hall or lofty dome: the good, the true, the tender, these form the wealth of home. - Sarah J. Hale
- Where thou art, that, is home. - Emily Dickinson
- You see much more of your children once they leave home. - Lucille Ball

New Home

- Bless this home with lots of love, may angels guide you from above.
- Bless your new home, may it be a place of beautiful memories for years to come.
- Congratulations on your new home.
- Fill it with joy and sweetness within every wall.
- Four walls may make a house but love makes a home.
- God Bless this home so full of love.
- Happy Housewarming!
- Happy in heart and home is the family that prays together.
- He is happiest, be he king or peasant, who finds peace in his home. - Johann von Goethe
- Home is where your heart is. May yours ever be full with love.
- Home Sweet Home for you, me and baby makes three.

- Junk is something you've kept for years and throw away three weeks before you need it.
- Love built this house.
- May it be a blessing to all who visit.
- May you find new blessings and joy in your new home.
- Today is a special day as we celebrate making your new house a home.
- We are so excited for you on your new home.
- Where your heart is there is your treasure.
- Wow-A new beginning!
- Your home is your castle, may you feel like royalty and know that you are rich in love.

Congratulations on your new space
It's small but it's all your place!

The pitter-patter of little feet
The scent of honeysuckle, oh how sweet
Laughing and thumping is heard in the hall
The dog's a barkin' and a bouncing ball
The wash is blowing in the breeze
All in our new home is at ease.
– GG Milam

A Big Congratulations To the Both of You

On purchasing your new home, you've made your dream come true!
Of course there's always things that you now will have to do
To keep the place looking swell for instance, here's a few:
Like mowing grass on weekends and repairing doors that stick
Painting walls and ceilings–what colors will you pick?
Hedges may need clipping a porch that will need swept
Don't want your neighbors griping if the place should look unkept!
But in the end it's worth it 'cause nothing else can beat
The pride you're gonna feel as the best house on the street!
– Jennifer Byerly

HUMOR

- A clear conscience is usually the sign of a bad memory.
- A conclusion is the place where you got tired of thinking.
- A day without sunshine is like–night.
- All the world's a stage, and I missed rehearsal.
- Baldness is a cure for dandruff.
- Before you criticize someone, walk a mile in their shoes. Then, you'll be a mile from them, and have their shoes.
- Behind every successful woman is a sink full of dishes, basket of laundry and freezer full of fast food.
- Bills travel through the mail at twice the speed of checks.
- Change is inevitable... except from vending machines.
- Deadline for all complaints was yesterday.
- Did you ever notice that people who are late are often much jollier than the people who have to wait for them?
- Duct tape is like the force. It has a light side and a dark side, and it holds the universe together.
- Eagles may soar, but weasels don't get sucked into jet engines
- Every time I close the door on reality it comes back in through the windows.
- Experience is something you don't get until just after you need it.
- Give a man a fish and he will eat for a day. Teach him to use the internet and he won't bother you for weeks.
- Going to church doesn't make you a Christian any more than standing in a garage makes you a car.
- He, who laughs last, thinks slowest.
- Honk, if you love peace and quiet.
- I drive way too fast to worry about cholesterol.

I hope life isn't a big joke, because I don't get it.

- I intend to live forever–so far, so good.
- I just got lost in thought–it was unfamiliar territory.
- I only feel stress at two times...day and night.
- I try to take one day at a time, but sometimes several days attack me at once.
- I wonder how much deeper the ocean would be without sponges.
- If everything seems to be going well, you have obviously overlooked something.
- If I knew what I was doing, it wouldn't be called "research."
- If it breaks, make it bigger–if it sticks out, chrome it.
- If you are grouchy, irritable, or just plain mean, there will be a $100 charge for putting up with you.
- If you think nobody cares about you, try missing a couple of payments.
- Laugh and the world laughs with you.
- Life is like an ice cream cone... just when you think you've got it licked, it drips on you.
- Life is uncertain. Eat dessert first.
- Monday is an awful way to spend 1/7th of your life.
- My truck does not leak–it's marking it's territory.
- Never do card tricks for the group you play poker with.
- Never take life seriously. Nobody gets out alive, anyway.
- No one is listening until you make a mistake.
- Normal is just a setting on the dryer.
- On the keyboard of life, always keep one finger on the escape key.
- On the other hand... we have different fingers.
- One good turn gets most of the blankets.

The hardness of the butter is directly proportional to the softness of the bread.

- ◉ The rooster crows but the hen delivers the goods.
- ◉ The severity of the itch is inversely proportional to the ability to reach it.
- ◉ The sooner you fall behind, the more time you'll have to catch up.
- ◉ When confronted by a difficult problem, you can solve it more easily by reducing it to the question, "How would the Lone Ranger handle this?"
- ◉ When everything's coming your way, you're in the wrong lane and going the wrong way.
- ◉ When you are dissatisfied and would like to go back to youth, think of algebra.
- ◉ Work when you should and play all the time.
- ◉ Wouldn't it be nice if, whenever we messed up our life, we could simply press "Ctrl Alt Delete" and start all over?
- ◉ You can't have everything! Where would you put it?
- ◉ You have the right to remain silent. Anything you say will be misquoted, then used against you.

Was today really necessary?

My face in the mirror
Isn't wrinkled or drawn.
My house isn't dirty
The cobwebs are gone.
My garden looks lovely
And so does my lawn.
I think I might never
Put my glasses back on...

As the light changed from red to green to yellow and back to red again, I sat there thinking about life. Is that what life is? Nothing more than a bunch of honking and yelling?

Sung to the tune of
"My Country Tis Of Thee"
My candy 'tis of thee
Sweet end to misery
Of thee I'll eat
Melt on thy tongue of mine
So good and quite divine
From every candy store
Of thee I sing-
– Jennifer Byerly

Lonely Socks.com

I wonder where the socks go
When the wash is done
You start out with a pair
But end with only one

Some say the washer eats them
But I don't think that's so
Still I have no idea
Where the heck they go!

So I've started a new service
Called lonely socks.com
With pictures and profiles
To reflect and look upon!

So if you're hunting for a sock
Please don't hesitate
To dial up my service
And I'll find you a "sole" mate!
– Jennifer Byerly

I saw this guy riding his bike. He was sweating heavily and his hair was blowing through the air. He was going about 50 mph! I started wondering what those straps were around his bike, then I wondered why he was on top of a car. I guess that could explain how fast he was going.
– Lara LaTourelle

JUST BECAUSE

Sometimes a friend will enter
Our lives though not for long
And then there comes a time
When you find you've both moved on

Because sometimes with friendships
Like seasons do not last
If only for awhile
'Twill soon become the past

So if you can be wise
And realize that everyone
Has had a piece in shaping
The person you've become

Then you will be much richer
From all you've had to gain
From all the friends who fade
And all who still remain
– Jennifer Byerly

The gift of a good friend is something
I'm certain can never be bought
It's the way that you choose to treat others
And the goodness in you that is sought
Yes, the joy found in friendship is something
That no tangible thing can contain
When the bows and the wrapping are missing
It is friendship that always remains
So I'm wrapping our friendship then binding
It close to the core of my heart
So I can remember it always
In case we are ever apart!
– Jennifer Byerly

If laughter were a tonic,
I'm sure it would be true
That I would be the healthiest
When I spend time with you!
– Jennifer Byerly

Just because you're special
Just because you're you,
You make people happy
With what you say and do.
– Sharon Ezzell

God filled our world with
Beauty animals and birds on wing,
Today may they be all around
You and may your happy heart sing.
– Sharon Ezzell

May the wonder of our world
Lift your heart today,
And may all of it's beauty find
You each step of the way.
– Sharon Ezzell

Blessings to You

God's handiwork is everywhere in
The mountains and the plains,
When the sun is shining
And even when it rains.

I hope as you go about the
Things you must do today,
That God's handiwork is evident
With little blessings along the way.
– Sharon Ezzell

Hello

I'm sending this card to you
Just to say hello
I think you're really great and
Wanted to tell you so!
– Thena Smith

The Face in the Mirror

Pick up this mirror and take a look
Tell me what you see
Can you see the one within
Whom others strive to be?

Your sunny outlook in this life
Has others looking too
To view the world as you see it
In the special way you do

The mirror shows no cracks
Nor dulling of your shine
It glows of warmth and kindness
Unchanging throughout time

Now gaze upon the lives you've touched
Take pride in all you've done
The extension of your hand and heart
Accepting everyone

Remember when you see the glass
The sparkle that you give
A reflection of God's goodness
It's just the way you live!
– Jennifer Byerly

*Just because I'm thinking of you today
I'm sending this little card your way!*

KiDS WiSDOM

- ◎ Ask for sprinkles and a cherry on top. - Hannah, age 8
- ◎ Cowboys don't take baths, they just dust off. - Neil, age 6
- ◎ Daddy, Me and sister are going to marry you when we get older. - Katelyn, age 5
- ◎ How do I love thee when you're always picking your nose? - Austin, age 14
- ◎ I am in love with you most of the time, but don't bother me when I'm with my friends. - Jon, age 13
- ◎ I did not bite my sister. It was a bee. - Nathaniel, age 4
- ◎ I heard that love is the most important thing in the world, but basketball is pretty good too. - Stephen, age 12
- ◎ I'm not a lyin'! I'm an elephant! - Katie age 4, caught telling a lie
- ◎ If you want a dog, start by asking for a horse. - Jackson, age 9
- ◎ If your going to draw on the wall, do it behind the couch and with a permanent marker... so it will last. - Emma, age 5
- ◎ I'm in favor of love as long as it doesn't happen when my favorite show is on television. - Randy, age 11
- ◎ I'm not rushing into being in love... I'm finding fourth grade hard enough. - Lisa, age 9
- ◎ It's more fun to color outside the lines. - Pam, age 15
- ◎ Love is great, especially the candy and flowers on Valentines. - Cheryl, age 10
- ◎ Love is gross! It gives you cooties! - Keyon, age 12
- ◎ Me says, "Mom, why can't I? It's a free country." Mom says, "Not while you're under my roof, it's not." - Lee, age 10
- ◎ Mommy where is God? In Heaven? I want to see Him right now! - Lynn age 3
- ◎ Mommy, God must be the moon because Jesus is the Son. - Natalie age 3 1/2, looking at the moon smiling down at her
- ◎ There is no good reason why clothes have to match. - Ed, age 11

KINDNESS

- A kind word is like a Spring day. - Russian Proverb
- A man never stands as tall as when he kneels to help a child. - Knights of Pythagoras
- Guard well within yourself that treasure, kindness.
- How beautiful a day can be when kindness touches it!
- I expect to pass through this world but once. Any good therefore that I can do, or any kindness or abilities that I can show to any fellow creature, let me do it now. Let me not defer it or neglect it, for I shall not pass this way again. - William Penn
- Kindness is more important than wisdom, and the recognition of this is the beginning of wisdom.
- Know how to give without hesitation, how to lose without regret, how to acquire without meanness. - George Sand
- Sometimes someone says something really small, and it just fits right into this empty place in your heart.
- The best portion of a good man's life is his little nameless, unremembered acts of kindness and of love. - W. Wordsworth
- Those who bring sunshine to the lives of others cannot keep it from themselves. Your kindness has warmed my heart so.
- Those who plant kindness harvest love.

Have you had a kindness shown?
Pass it on;
'Twas not given for thee alone,
Pass it on;
Let it travel down the years,
Let it wipe another's tears,
'Til in Heaven the deed appears.

KWANZAA

- A celebration of family, community, & culture.
- A Recommitment of Faith
- Celebrate a new beginning
- Let us celebrate our rich heritage.
- Let's celebrate today!
- Observe our history, our precious heritage.
- Rejoice in the season
- Sharing Kwanzaa with you
- Wish you happiness at Kwanzaa time.
- With a commitment of family and faith

May you feel the peace this season
Warmest wishes for happy holidays
Sending you love this Kwanzaa
As you light the candles-Celebrate

May today be a reflection of pride
for generations to come.
May we unify our hearts and families
as we look forward to
tomorrow and a brighter future.
- CC Milam

Today we come together as a family
To echo our forefathers and their
Commitment to tradition and history.
~ CC Milam

The Seven Principles (Nguzo Saba) of Kwanzaa

Umoja (oo-MOH-jah):
Unity
Success starts with Unity. Unity of family,
community, nation and race.

Kujichagulia (koo-jee-chah-goo-LEE-ah):
Self-Determination
To be responsible for ourselves. To create your own destiny.

Ujima (oo-JEE-mah):
Collective work and responsibility
To build and maintain your community together. To work
together to help one another within your community.

Ujamaa (oo-jah-MAH):
Collective economics
To build, maintain, and support our own stores,
establishments, and businesses.

Nia (NEE-ah):
Purpose
To restore African American people to their traditional
greatness. To be responsible to Those Who Came Before (our
ancestors) and to Those Who Will Follow (our descendants).

Kuumba (koo-OOM-bah):
Creativity
Using creativity and imagination to make your
communities better than what you inherited.

Imani (ee-MAH-nee):
Faith
Believing in our people, our families, our educators, our leaders,
and the righteousness of the African American struggle.

LOSS

I think you know how sad we are
I think you know we care
And each joy or sadness in your life
We as your best friends share.

Job

So sorry to hear of your loss
But at least you're rid of
That mean 'ole boss!
Hope you find a new job soon.

Pet

When we take on a pet, we all know that
One day we must tell them good-bye.
It's hard but still we must do it–
Though at times, we may question why...
I pray that your memories sustain you
With a joy in every sort of way.
May they always serve to remind you
How your friend made you smile each day!
– Jennifer Byerly

Friendship

Please know that my thoughts are with you
And I pray that you'll always depend
On the memories that will always be with you
As you work through the loss of your friendship.
– Jennifer Byerly

May the Lord comfort you at this
time as only He can do.

LOVE

- As deep as the ocean, as huge as the sky, you are the apple of my eye. – GG Milam
- At the touch of love, everyone becomes a poet. – Plato
- By these words may you always know that my love is with you wherever you go.
- Come live with me and be my love, and we will some new pleasures prove, of golden sands, and crystal beaches, with silken lines and silver hooks. – John Donne
- Dance with me darling, ever so slow. Hold my love in your heart and never let go. – LaTourelle
- Every theory of love, from Plato down, teaches that each individual loves in the other sex what he lacks in himself. – G. Stanley Hall
- Falling in love is when you lay in his arms and wake up in your dreams.
- How delicious is the winning of a kiss at love's beginning. – T. Campbell
- I will not love you for the rest of your life, but for the rest of mine.
- If I could reach up and hold a star for every time you made me smile, I would have the whole night sky in the palm of my hand.
- If I had a flower for every time I thought of you, I could walk in my garden forever. – Alfred Lord Tennyson
- If the Sea were of ink and the sky were of paper I could still not begin to describe my love for you.
- If you live to be a hundred, I want to live to be a hundred minus one day, so I never have to live without you.
- If you say my eyes are beautiful it's because they're looking at you.
- Knowing you'll be in all my tomorrows, makes my today so wonderful!
- Let us dance with joy so sweet, for in the twinkling of our feet, our spirit and our soul doth meet. – LaTourelle

- Life has taught us that love does not consist in gazing at each other, but in looking outward together in the same direction. - Antoine de Saint-Exupery

- Love is honest. Love is true. Love is what carries us through... - August Jones

- Love is what's left in a relationship after all the selfishness has been removed. - Cullen Hightower

- No matter what, no matter where, you take me with you everywhere... - August Jones

- Once he drew, with one long kiss my whole soul through my lips. - Tennyson

- One does not perceive the joy of a green leaf until wintertime comes and there are none-like a love.

- One word frees us of all the weight and pain in life, that word is love. - Sophocles

- Sometimes your nearness takes my breath away; and all the things I want to say can find no voice. Then, in silence, I can only hope my eyes will speak my heart. - Robert Sexton

- The heart has its reasons that reason knows nothing of. - Blaise Pascal

- The most precious possession that ever comes to a man in this world is a woman's heart.

- The soul that can speak through the eyes can also kiss with a gaze. - LaTourelle

- The sweetest things that your lips shall touch are mine. - Peachez

- There is no remedy for love than to love more. - Henry David Thoreau

- What a grand thing, to be loved! What a grander thing still, to love! - Victor Hugo

- What I do and what I dream include thee, as the wine must taste of its own grapes. - Elizabeth Barret Browning

- What I feel for you seems less of earth and more of a cloudless heaven. - Victor Hugo

- When I look into your eyes I see the love that God has given me.

Touch my life with tenderness
And fill my cup with love.
Share my dreams as I share
Yours beyond the stars above.
'Tis you that doth my heart belong
And you I love 'til day is done
How blessed is my love for thee
That I may ever sing joyfully
– LaTourelle

The way that you love me
is such music divine
Like that old favorite song
one hears in their mind
Singing sweet, singing soft,
over and over again
With a rhapsody that rings
to the depths of my soul
For my love you are
the orchestra of life so full
Play me slow, play me gentle,
never let go...
– LaTourelle

How do I love thee?
Let me count the ways ~
Hmm, I start with one, right?
~ CC Milam

How I have loved thee? With all that I am,
Joy fills my heart since this love began.
Would that I could give you all that I am,
Love lives within me yet more and again.
– LaTourelle

Say that you love me
Say that it's true
Know that it matters
because I love you.

'Tis you that doth my heart belong
And you I love 'til day is done
How blessed is my love for thee
That I may ever sing joyfully
– LaTourelle

You made the whole world look brighter
And made me love literature and art
For everything seems more wonderful
With so much love in my heart.
– Thena Smith

Do I love you? Do I love you?
Does the sun still shine?
Do the stars still twinkle?

White puffy clouds that go sailing by
I see as I look up in the baby blue sky
Remind me of special days gone by
Memories of the past come pouring in
My thoughts flow to you once again
And reveal to me how our love did begin.
– GG Milam

You are the answer ~ Love is the question

Thanks for memories and blessings you give me throughout
my days. For standing close beside me in such immeasurable
ways. You are my knight in shining armor and I your maid sweet
and fair. Your devotion is to me a love beyond compare.

Who am I without you—
Sugar without sweet
Sails without wind
Sand with no sea
Simply put
Love alone

You Are

The sparkle in my eye
Better than strawberry pie
Mittens when it's cold
A treasure worth more than gold
The rhapsody in spring
More precious than anything
Laughter in the sun
Dreams when day is done
All this and so much more
Is everything that I adore

There are no words that tell
The love I have for you
The depths of my feelings
Extend beyond imagination

I want to hold thee in this warmth forever
To feel thy breath encompass me
The rhythm of thy heart doth revive my very soul
Passion ignites fervently within my being,
As thee entwined thy body around mine
The intimate grasp from thy touch
Has captured all that I am
- LaTourelle

Greater love has no one than this, that he lay down his life for his friends.
— John 15:13 NIV

My bounty is as boundless as the sea, my love is deep, the more I give to thee the more I have, for both are infinite.
— William Shakespeare

Love is like tiny grains of sand... if you hold it tightly within your hand, it will seep through the cracks of your fingers, but if you hold it gently and softly, it will remain.

Love is the irresistible desire to be irresistibly desired.

If I could come back as anything, It would be as one of your tears. How could I want more than to be conceived in your heart, Born in your eyes, Live on your cheeks and die on your lips...

See there's this place in me where your fingerprints still rest, your kisses still linger, and your whispers softly echo. It's the place where a part of you will forever be a part of me.
— Gretchen Kemp

From every human being there rises a light that reaches straight to heaven. And when two souls that are destined to be together find each other, their streams of light flow together, and a single brighter light goes forth from their united being.

Today I found love ~ Today... I found you!

My love is like a red red rose
That's newly sprung in June;
My love is like the melody
that's sweetly played in tune.
– Robert Burns

I send you a cream-white rosebud
With a flush upon its petal tips;
For the love that is purest and sweetest
Has a kiss of desire on the lips.
– John Boyle O'Reilly

'Twas a new feeling-something more
than we had dared to own before
Which when we hid not;
We saw in each other's eye,
And wished, in every half-breathed sigh,
To speak, but did not.
– Thomas Moore

My bounty is as boundless as the sea,
My Love is deep,
The more I give to thee the more I have,
For both are infinite.
~ William Shakespeare

The way that you love me is such music divine
Like that old favorite song one hears in their mind
Singing sweet, singing soft, over and over again
With a rhapsody that rings to the depths of my soul
For my love you are the orchestra of life so full
Play me slow, play me gentle, never let go
– LaTourelle

Perhaps Love

Perhaps love is like a resting place, a shelter from the storm
It exists to give you comfort, it is there to keep you warm
In those times of trouble when you are most alone
The memory of love will bring you home...
If I should live forever and all my dreams come true
My memories of love will be of you.
– John Denver

And in Life's noisiest hour,
There whispers still the ceaseless Love of Thee,
The heart's Self-solace and soliloquy.
You mould my Hopes, you fashion me within;
And to the leading Love-throb in the Heart
Thro' all my Being, thro' my pulse's beat;
You lie in all my many Thoughts, like Light,
Like the fair light of Dawn, or summer Eve
On rippling Stream, or cloud-reflecting Lake.
And looking to the Heaven, that bends above you,
How oft! I bless the Lot that made me love you.
– Samuel Taylor Coleridge

If ever two were one, then surely we.
If ever man were lov'd by wife, then thee;
If ever wife was happy in a man,
Compare with me ye women if you can.
I prize thy love more then whole mines of gold,
Or all the riches that the East doth hold.
My love is such that rivers cannot quench,
Nor ought but love from thee, give recompense.
Thy love is such I can no way repay,
The heavens reward thee manifold I pray.
Then while we live, in love let's so persevere,
That when we live no more, we may live ever.
– Anne Bradstreet

You are to me the rainbow through the rain
You bring the calm before the storm
You are to me the laughter through the pain
You fill my life with everything warm

*A bit of fragrance always clings to the
hand that gives roses.* ~ Chinese Proverb

Because of the Lord's great love we are not consumed,
for His compassions never fail. They are new every morning;
great is your faithfulness. – Lamentations 3:22-23 NIV

I am come that they might have life, and that they might
have it more abundantly. I am the good shepherd: the good
shepherd giveth His life for the sheep. – John 10:10-11 NIV

Love the Lord your God with all your heart and with all your
soul and with all your mind and with all our strength.
– Mark 12:30 NIV

*Out of all the treasures in the world there
is nothing more precious than giving
someone a piece of your heart.*

For God so loved the world, that He gave
His only begotten Son, that whosoever believeth
in Him should not perish, but have everlasting life.
For God sent not His Son into the world to
condemn the world; but that the world
through Him might be saved.
– John 3:16-17
KJV

Memorial Day

- All we have of freedom, all we use or know–this our fathers bought for us long and long ago. - Rudyard Kipling

- Although no sculptured marble should rise to their memory, nor engraved stone bear record of their deeds, yet will their remembrance be as lasting as the land they honored. - Daniel Webster

- But the freedom that they fought for, and the country grand they wrought for, is their monument to-day, and for aye. - Thomas Dunn English

- Death leaves a heartache no one can heal, love leaves a memory no one can steal. - From a headstone in Ireland

- For death is no more than a turning of us over from time to eternity. - William Penn

- How important it is for us to recognize and celebrate our heroes and she-roes! - Maya Angelou

- Who kept the faith and fought the fight; The glory theirs, the duty ours. - Wallace Bruce

God's blessing be upon us
As we take this special day
To remember those that touched us
Yet now have passed away
Let no one be neglectful
Or let an evening pass
Without remembering loved ones
With prayers that will last
- Jennifer Byerly

Cover them over with beautiful flowers,
Deck them with garlands, those brothers of ours,
Lying so silent by night and by day
Sleeping the years of their manhood away.
- Will Carleton

MEMORIES

Memories of Dad

My Daddy was a hard working man.
You could tell by his rough callused hands.
He worked so hard from dawn till dusk.
In God above he put his trust.
I loved to walk by Daddy's side.
In his eyes, I saw pride.
He always did the best he could
To see that life for his family was good.
— Linda Zimmerman

When Do Yesterdays Start

When do yesterdays start and tomorrows end
When the past seems like a long lost friend
Back in time before we were alone
The house used to breathe with laughter and song
When the children came in and brought friends along
Waiting up for them to get home from a date
Was the last time we stayed up late
The phone sits silent, no one calls anymore
The bell doesn't ring, no knock on the door
The rooms stay tidy; everything's in its place
I stare at the pictures resting on the bookcase
As we sit and remember the good times we had
Funny how good times can suddenly feel sad
The children have gone to make their own ways
But, we still see them on the holidays
We sit on the porch with a cup of tea
And reminisce how things used to be
When do yesterdays start and tomorrows end
If only life could be as it was back then.
— Barbara Cox

With the smell of honeysuckle
I remember days gone by–
I was jumping fences
My how time does fly–

We do not remember days.
We remember moments.

Remember days of youth–
Sweet Innocence
Remember when the weight of the
world was light as a feather–
– GG Milam

Old Friends

Wandering back through the rivers of time
As special memories fill my mind
People and places that once meant so much
Now we rarely even keep in touch
We went to your house you came to our home
So long ago before the children were grown
We went out for dinner even danced a few
The secrets we shared between me and you
I took a walk through the old neighborhood
The houses now making their own memories
Raising their children sowing their seeds
Although we have parted and went our own ways
I sometimes journey back to the days
To you my friend, I'll lift my glass
As long as there's memories,
friendships will last!
– Barbara Cox

When someone you love becomes a memory...
The memory becomes a treasure.

MILITARY

- ◉ Brave Solider
- ◉ Thank you for serving our country
- ◉ Thank you for the price of freedom
- ◉ Words can not express my deepest gratitude for you
- ◉ You make a difference in the life of our country
- ◉ Your favorite colors are Red, White & Blue

Missing Daddy

I really miss my daddy.
He's away at war.
I miss the sound of his footsteps,
Coming through the door.
I know he's serving our country,
And I'm so proud of him.
But I really miss my Daddy
And the fun I had with him.
I really miss my daddy.
I feel so all alone.
I pray that God will bring
My Daddy safely home.
– Linda Zimmerman

Son at War

We hoped the time would never come,
When at war we'd find our son.
We know he proudly our country serves,
And our honor he deserves.
We listen daily to the news,
And pray our son we will not lose.
Many have paid the highest price
So we can have a free life.
Our hearts are heavy as we hear,
Of other parents who have lost a dear son.
We pray for all in that far away land,
Fighting for a better day.
– Linda Zimmerman

I sure miss my Mommy
She's away at war.
I know it's in a land
That is so very far.
I miss her hugs and kisses
And all the things that Mommy's do.
I will be so very glad when this war is through.
I'm proud she serves our country
And stands for what is right,
But I really miss my Mommy
Tucking me in at night.
I'm counting off the days
Until her duty ends
And I pray each night for her
Until she's home again.
– Linda Zimmerman

Daddy, when you are gone out to sea
Our house is much too quiet for me.
And we don't laugh as much during the day
At the funny things people say.
We don't giggle so much out loud
But we do try to make you proud
By helping Mom and being good
Just the way you said we should.
When you are gone on deployment
It takes away from our enjoyment
Of anything that we love to do
For Daddy we are incomplete...without you.
We try hard to be so very brave
And every e-mail we all save
And every photo, every word
And telephone message that we heard.
I store it all within my heart
The whole time that we're apart
And when you get back home again
My heart will wear a great big grin!
– Thena Smith

Homecoming

The waiting over the time is past.
Our soldier is coming home at last.
Our prayer has turned into a praise,
As to God our thanks we raise.
Hugs and kissed joyful tears,
As we let go of all our fears.
Time to share and share again
Things that happened since apart we've been.
Things have changed since we've been apart.
Yet, still unchanged is the love in our hearts.
Now together again,
With the love of family and friends,
We treasure each and everyday
And pray you are home to stay!

         – Linda Zimmerman

Freedom for our Country has a price for me.
My husband serving proudly way across the sea.
Often through the day he is in my prayers.
I pray that God will shelter
And keep him in His care.
E-mails and letters mean so much to me,
I'm counting off the days
Until his face I'll see.
Our little girl is growing without her Daddy by her side.
I send him pictures showing
All the things she does with pride.
As I rock my child whose Daddy is not here,
I tell her of his love
And wipe away a tear.
Each day I hear the news of the war so far away
I pause what I'm doing
And for my husband pray.
I hope that many others will join me
Each day remember our soldiers
And take time to pray.

         – Linda Zimmerman

MISSING YOU

- A thousand years, you said, as our hearts melted I look at the hand you held, and the ache is hard to bear. - Heguri

- Can you know the longing I feel when I am away from you?

- How can I miss you if you won't go away?

- I miss you and hope you come home soon.

- If I had a flower for every time I thought of you, I could walk in my garden forever. - Lord Tennyson

- It's hard to tell your mind to stop loving someone when your heart still does.

- Missing you–is missing love, missing life, missing breathing, missing everything... I hate missing...

- My heart is delicate, so be gentle. Do not far from me stay.

- So you are gone again and far away... The cat says she misses you and I guess you would be nicer to snuggle with than her...

- What can I say?? I MISS YOU!!!

- What I do and what I dream include thee, as the wine must taste of its own grapes. - Elizabeth Barrett Browning

- When I dream of you... I dream in color.

- Within you I lose myself. Without you I find myself wanting to become lost again.

To live in the hearts of those you leave behind is never to die. ~ Robert Orr

O happy hours when I may once more encircle within these arms the dearest object of my love- when I shall again feel the pressure of that "aching head" which will delight to recline upon my bosom, when I may again press to my heart which palpitates with the purest affection that loved one who has so long shared it's undivided devotion.
                                                    - Alexander Hamilton Rice

Today I awoke and looked around
But no sign of you I found
And then I remembered you were away
And so I'm missing you today!
– Thena Smith

No matter what
No matter where
You take me with
You everywhere...
~ August Jones

I arise from dreams of thee
In the first sweet sleep of night,
When the winds are breathing low,
And the stars are shining bright.
– Percy Byssthe Shelley

Day is Done
Gone the sun
From the lake From the hills
From the sky All is well
Safely rest God is nigh
Fading light dims the sight
And a star Gems the sky
Gleaming bright From afar
Drawing nigh Falls the night
– Major General Daniel Butterfield

See there's this place in me where your fingerprints still rest, your kisses still linger, and your whispers softly echo. It's the place where a part of you will forever be a part of me.
– Gretchen Kemp

MOThER's DAY

- A mother can sing the song of her child's heart, when they have long since forgotten.
- A mother is she who can take the place of all others but whose place no one else can take. - Cardinal Mermillod
- A mother understands what a child does not say.
- A mothers love is seen as she kneels by the bed of her child.
- As a mother comforts her child, so I will comfort you. - Isaiah 66:13 NIV
- Being a mother not only takes time, but also requires generous amounts of faith and courage.
- Earthly angels are mothers in disguise.
- God sends us to our mothers and places His love in their hearts for us. - CC Milam
- Her children arise up, and call her blessed. - Proverbs 31:28 KJV
- Motherhood is a joy and a gift from God.
- One knows that you are a special mom when you count the sprinkles on each cupcake to make sure they are equal
- There is no snooze button on a baby who wants breakfast. Congratulations on your 1st Mother's Day!
- You can fool some of the people all of the time and all of the people some of the time, but a Mom—never!

M-O-T-H-E-R

"M" is for the million things she gave me,
"O" means only that she's growing old,
"T" is for the tears she shed to save me,
"H" is for her heart of purest gold;
"E" is for her eyes, with love-light shining,
"R" means right, and right she'll always be,
Put them all together, they spell "MOTHER,"
A word that means the world to me.
- Howard Johnson

God made mother's special
With lots of loving care
He placed in her a tender heart
Forgiveness when we err
He fashioned her with goodness
Gentleness and light
A brightness in her smile
That could light the stars at night
But first God made a woman
His most famous work of art
Because you don't have to be a mother
To have a mother's heart
– Jennifer Byerly

Mother, you filled my days with fairytales
And my nights with sugar plum dreams
You held my hand for a while,
But my heart is yours forever...

For Mama 1918-1997

She saw the Master's touch in simple things:
a field of wild flowers after a gentle rain
a hued rainbow arched across the gray sky:
rare jewels a mortal's money can never buy.

A snowdrop peeking through the melting snow.
Many golden honey bees all flying to and fro.
The deep dark furrows of a rich loamy field.
Seeds, plentiful harvest, in time would yield.

The perfection and wonder of a newborn child.
Simple delight in watching her baby's smile.
The Seasons and changing color of the leaves
Mama saw the Master's touch in all of these
– Lottie Ann Knox

My mother gave me the best she had
She gave me all of her
And in the quietness of the night
Her prayers were lifted high for me
I must tell her just how wonderful she is
Her love is the greatest gift
And I am so blessed to call her Mother

It takes a special mother to make a house a home
To fill the rooms with laughter and never feel alone
I know I am so truly blessed to be the child of you
So on this day for mothers, I give my heart anew
May God pour out his love on this Mother's Day
                                    – LaTourelle

A pillar of strength, the pure meaning of Love
A Divine gift from our Lord up above
As gentle as rain on the petals of a rose
She'll kiss away fears and hug away woes
A doctor when tending a cold or a scrap
A chef when making cookies or frosting a cake
A tailor, a chauffeur, a fairy godmother at times
But never to busy for a child's nursery rhymes
A source of wisdom that comes from inside
A manager, a bookkeeper and a private tour guide
The one that knows just what to say
When a child is having a difficult day
The maker of dreams and the setter of goals
As a pile of laundry she sits and folds
When strange noises go bump in the night
It's her loving hand that turns on the light
All things to family she feels she must be
Although her family may not see
In our Lord's kingdom the one that will fare
Is the one we call Mother, No others compare!
                                    – Barbara K. Cox

To be a Mother is not just to have children.
One must love and protect their young
while they nurture and mold them.
To be a Mother is to have unconditional
love and many nights without sleep.
To be a Mother is to have the greatest
Joy in the world right at your feet.
Thank you Mother for your love and
Teaching me to be a great mother too.
                                    – GG Milam

Thank you Mother for the life you gave me.
Mother's Day is a wonderful time
To let you know my love for you.
For years your arms were empty longing for
A love to fill the empty space in your heart.
And then I was born–not of you but of another–
Your love for me was so great.
You loved and nurtured me as your own.
You held me close–and we became one.
Thank you for your love.
Thank you for being my mom.
May the Lord Bless you today on
The day of your birth and every day.
– GG Milam

As we age, we begin to realize the value of a mother's love and
the enormous depth of her commitment to us. No other
relationship we form can ever be as close or profound as
that with our mothers.

A picture memory brings to me; I look across the years
and see myself beside my mother's knee I feel her
gentle hand restrain my selfish moods, and know again
a child's blind sense of wrong and pain. But wiser now, a man
gray grown, my childhood needs are better known. My
mother's chastening love I owe.   – John Greenleaf Whittier

Mother

Who gave me life and held my hand
And caught me when I fell.
Who never failed to comfort me
When I was scared or ill.
Who gave so much and cheered me on
And cared with heart in hand.
Who will always be a part of me,
My mother, my dear friend.
No painter's brush, nor poet's pen
In justice to her fame
Has ever reached half high enough
To write a mother's name.
Because I feel that in the heavens above
The angels, whispering one to another,
Can find among their burning tears of love,
None so devotional as that of "Mother,"
Therefore, by that dear name I have long called you,
You who are more than mother unto me.
– Edgar Allan Poe

Best friends, forever mom and me
Picking flowers and climbing trees.
A shoulder to cry on secrets to share
Warm hearts and hands that really care.
I said a prayer on Mother's Day
to thank the Lord above
For giving me a lifetime full
Of your caring and your love.
I thank God for the sacrifice
You've made throughout the years,
For your tenderness and mercy
And chasing away my fears.
Youth fades; love droops,
The leaves of friendship fall;
A mother's secret hope outlives them all.
– Oliver Wendell Holmes

NaTURE

- ◎ All the flowers of all the tomorrows are in the seeds of today.
- ◎ He who would have nothing to do with thorns must never attempt to gather flowers.
- ◎ It takes both rain and sunshine to make a rainbow.
- ◎ Time is nature's way of preventing everything from happening at once.

My Little Stream

A little stream runs by our village
I don't know where it goes
But I want to follow its spillage
Through the rocks by the hedgerows
Like quicksilver it twists and turns
Through the down-land meadows
Bustling by the shrubs and ferns
Gurgling as it sparkles and flows
Under a bridge of wood or stone
Or it brushes past the cottage
Yonder standing amidst the fields alone
It meanders into the dark wood
And cannot be seen awhile
Till it emerges where the otters brood
And sparkles clearly for a mile
Then it meets the broad river
And merges its tiny might to the flow
And I wonder if you can ever feel it
There in the city below.
– Sumanta Sanyal

*Cool crisp air and piles of leaves
Make having fun a breeze.*
~ Linda Zimmerman

There's a tree in the garden
That bears no fruit
But its leaves are all golden
And it wears them like a suit
It stands and serves no purpose
Yet, Grandpa says it's his best
For beauty is as beauty does
And nature knows no waste.
– Sumanta Sanyal

All men are like grass,
and all their glory is like the
flowers of the field.
The grass withers and the flowers fall,
because the breath of the
LORD blows on them.
Surely the people are grass.
The grass withers and the flowers fall,
but the word of our God stands forever.
– Isaiah 40:6-8 NIV

The Dandelion

How sweet to see a dandelion
In the hands of a little girl
She delights in the simple things
That grow for free in our world

Wishers she calls them
And she blows the bloom away
Hoping that her wishes come true
Before another day

How lovely to be so innocent
So adorable and so sweet
And depend upon the dandelion
For a wonderful playtime treat.
– Thena Smith

NEW YEAR

A new year is upon us
Let's leave the last behind
Opportunity awaits us
Success is ours to find
Forget about past failures
Just toss them all away
Let's help all our tomorrows
By living well today!
– Jennifer Byerly

As a New Year Comes

One last road to travel...
one last way to go.
One more day to forever...
just to let you know.
The wait is finally over...
the journey now is through.
And now this comes to let you know...
dreams really do come true.
It's finally here Happy New Year

Happy New Year

Happy New Year to family
Happy New Year to friends
May you each enjoy the blessings
That our Lord God sends
And trust in His guidance all along the way
As you begin a brand new year on this happy day!
– Thena Smith

Today we celebrate with you
The beginning of a year brand new!

PETS

Congratulations on Becoming a Cat Owner

Father God in heaven
I lift my paws in prayer
In hopes that my new owner
Would stroke my soft brown hair
And may I always have a
Warm and welcome lap
Whenever I am wanting
To take a little nap
Let there be a kind hand
To scratch me on my head
And may there be a pillow plumped
That I can call my bed
And Father may I ask just
One more thing of you?
I'd sure be mighty thankful
For a tender mouse to chew!
– Jennifer Byerly

Best Wishes with Your New Puppy

You are my best friend
And I love you so very much!
I love the sound of your voice
And oh, how I love your touch!
I love it when you pat my head
And when you rub my belly
And when you play ball with me
My heart turns into jelly!
Although there may be some things
That I can't understand
I understand enough to know
That a pup's best friend is MAN!
– Thena Smith

PRAISE

Try a word of praise to anyone you love. Watch them give you more than they ever did before. Everyone is needing to know that they matter. So write a little note and share a special word. Try one or more of these and bless someone.

- A Big Hug
- A Big Kiss
- A Pat on the Back
- A Wink to You
- Awesome
- Bravo
- Dynamic
- Excellent
- Exceptional
- Fantastic
- God Bless You
- Good For You
- Good Idea
- Good Job
- Great
- Great Discovery
- High Five
- Hip, Hip, Hooray
- Hooray for you
- Hot Diggity Dog
- How Nice
- How Smart
- Hurray For You

- I Admire You
- I Have Fun with You
- I Knew You Could Do It
- I Like You
- I Love You!
- I Love Your Smile!
- I Respect You
- I Trust You
- I'm Amazed
- I'm Proud Of You
- Jesus Loves You
- Looking Good
- Love you bunches
- Lovely
- Magnificent
- Marvelous
- Neat
- Nice Work
- Nothing Can Stop You
- Outstanding Performance
- Remarkable
- Right
- Sensational

- Shine On
- Spectacular
- Super Job
- Super Star
- Super Work
- Terrific
- That's Correct
- That's Incredible
- That's Perfect
- That's the Way
- Way to Go
- Well Done
- What a Good Listener
- What an Imagination
- Wow
- You are a Blessing
- You are Exciting
- You are Loved
- You are Responsible
- You are the World to Me
- You Belong
- You Brighten My Day
- You Did It!

- You Make Me Happy
- You Sparkle
- You Tried Hard
- You're a Darling
- You're a Good Friend
- You're a Joy
- You're a Treasure
- You're a Winner
- You're Beautiful
- You're Fantastic
- You're Growing Up
- You're Important
- You're Incredible
- You're On Your Way
- You're Perfect
- You're Priceless
- You're Precious
- You're Sensational
- You're Special
- You're The Best
- You're Unique
- You're Wonderful
- You've Got a Friend

*No matter what, when,
why, where, or how...
All the things you do
make me say "W-O-W"*

PRAYERS

- A day started with prayer, rarely ever unravels.
- He who kneels before God can stand before anyone!
- Help is just a prayer away!
- I have not stopped giving thanks for you, remembering you in my prayers. - Ephesians 1:16 NIV
- Just sent you a knee-mail!
- Just do your best, Pray that it's blessed, and He'll take care of the rest.
- Life is fragile. Handle with prayer.
- Sometimes God calms the storms and sometimes He lets the storm rage and calms His child. May you feel the wave of His love embracing you with peace.
- The battle is on our knees before the Lord and the victory is all to His honor and His glory.
- The best we can give our children are our prayers. - GG Milam
- The Prayer of Jabez: Oh, that You would bless me and enlarge my territory! Let Your hand be with me, and keep me from harm so that I will be free from pain. - I Chronicles 4:10 NIV
- Until now you have not asked for anything in my name. Ask and you will receive, and your joy will be complete. - John 16:24 NIV
- We give thanks to God always for you all, making mention of you in our prayers. - I Thessalonians 1:2 KJV
- When at night you can not sleep, talk to the Shepherd and stop counting sheep.

Jesus' prayer for all His children: My prayer is not for them alone. I pray also for those who will believe in me through their message, that all of them may be one, Father, just as you are in me and I am in you. May they also be in us so that the world may believe that you have sent me.

- John 17:20-21 NIV

The Wonder of it All

I stand in awe before you, Lord
As I watch my child at play.
How precious is each action
and each word I hear him say.
I know that as You look down on us
We are so very small.
Yet, You know each tiny grain of sand
and by name you know us all!
Lord, though my child seems small to me
as he stands upon your shore,
I know that were he ten feel tall-
You could not love him more.
I cannot even fathom Lord,
How great your love must be
but I know that it is greater still
than the vastness of your sea.
I stand in humble reverence Lord
As I watch my child in play
and know that you watch over me
in much the self same way!
And so I say a prayer of thanks
Dear Lord of earth and sea
for all the loving care you give
to both my child and me.
– Thena Smith

I pray that God will lead me
Down paths so that I may
Be a humble servant
Each and every day
~ Jennifer Byerly

Take Time

Whether at the close
Or start of every day
Put your hands together
And take the time to pray
God is always listening
God is always there
Whenever you decide
To say a little prayer
— Jennifer Byerly

My Prayer for You

I will lift your name to God
Each time I stop to pray
I'll ask His grace and goodness
To follow you each day
And peace and joy and love
And light when you feel dim
Be still and know He's your God
And draw your strength from Him!
— Jennifer Byerly

Communion Prayer

Today is very special
As I bow my head to pray
To consider how God makes
A difference in my day
Without His son I'm nothing
And by grace I know I live
And I'm forever humbled
Of that which he forgives
The bread is Christ within me
The wine so sweet and pure
His blood meant to remind
Of all He did endure
— Jennifer Byerly

PROM

- All dressed up and ready to go
- Dance the night away
- Lady in red
- Making memories with forever friends
- Sharp dressed man
- To a beautiful lady
- To a handsome man

You are all dressed up from head to toe
As off to your prom you go.
You look so beautiful with your smile so sweet
And in this world you are amazingly unique
Enjoy your night and the memory will be dear
As you look back year after year.
– Thena Smith

Tonight is one more step into adulthood
And I must let you go...
You are not the little girl in dress-up clothes
Dancing around on her tippy toes...
You're all grown up and going off
To prom on your senior night...
– GG Milam

You are a lady dressed in sparkles and heels–a beautiful sight!
Hope you have a wonderful evening with your friends
Making memories until the evening ends.
– GG Milam

You stand before me as a handsome young man
With a beautiful lady holding your hand.
You're off to the prom with memories to make
You look wonderful–You and your date.
– GG Milam

RETIREMENT

Now as you retire
Take the time to be with family
Have fun, keep active
Make new friends
Kick your heels up
Throw out the clock

Yesterday I was working so hard
And at the end of the day
I was exhausted and TIRED.
But today the sun can rise and set
And I can remember
Or I can forget.
I can get up if I've had enough sleep
Or go back to bed
And count some more sheep.
I can get dressed and go out
Or stay in my jammies all day
Clean my house or go out and play.
I can dine on peanut butter and jelly
Or toast and muffins
Or I can buy lunch and cook nuthin'.
Oh, how wonderful just adding a "RE"
In front of "Tired"
Can make your world be!!
– Thena Smith

Happy Retirement
Now you can catch up on those naps.
Think of the long lunch breaks
Time for some R & R

ROMANCE

Are flowers the winter's choice?
Is love's bed always snow?
She seemed to hear my silent voice,
Not love's appeals to know
I never saw so sweet a face
As that I stood before
My heart has left its dwelling-place
And can return no more

Doubt that the stars are fire; doubt that
The sun doth move; doubt truth to be a
Liar, but never doubt that I love
~ Shakespeare

I gently touched her hand: she gave
A look that did my soul enslave:
I pressed her rebel lips in vain:
They rose up to be pressed again
Thus happy, I no farther meant,
Than to be pleased and innocent

Give me a kiss, add to that kiss a score:
Then to that twenty, add a hundred more:
A thousand to that hundred: so kiss on,
To make that thousand up a million
Treble that million, and when that is done,
Let's kiss afresh, as when we first begun
– Robert Herrick

Sensual pleasure passes in the twinkling of an eye, but the
friendship between us, the mutual confidence, the delights
of the heart, the enchantment of the soul, these things do not
perish and can never be destroyed I shall love you until I die.
– Voltaire

◉ Anyone can be passionate, but it takes real lovers to be silly. Thanks for being outrageously hysterical!

◉ Can I have your picture so I can show Santa what I want for Christmas?

◉ Come live with me, and be my love and we will all the pleasures prove. - Christopher Marlowe

◉ For as many times as the waves caress the shore, that's how much I love you.

◉ I am your canvas–paint me with your love.

◉ I believe in long, slow, deep, soft, wet kisses that last...

◉ I believe in the sun, even when it is not shining; in love... even when I am alone, and in God, even when he is silent.

◉ I only thought about you once today–I just never stopped.

◉ I found the one my soul loves, I held him and would not let him go. - Song of Solomon

◉ Love distills desire upon the eyes, love brings bewitching grace into the heart. -Euripides

◉ My love is like a tattered rose pressed into the pages of time. Each time a page is turned the memories flood back in, reminding me of a love so grand when once I was so young...

◉ Other men it is said have seen angels, but I have seen thee and thou art enough. - George Moore

◉ Some Enchanted Evening

◉ The very first moment I beheld him, my heart was irrevocably gone. -Jane Austen

◉ Thou art to me a delicious torment. - Ralph Waldo Emerson

◉ To the rose of my heart–I Love You.

◉ When I listen to my heart...it whispers your name.

◉ Whenever I think of perfect things, you're the first one that comes to my mind.

◉ Your kisses set my heart on fire.

Seasons

- A crisp Winter's breeze.
- A rainbow of colors all on the ground.
- As melodious robin redbreast awakens me with his call.
- Even when it's cold outside our memories will keep us warm. Want to snuggle???
- In the Good Ol' Summertime...
- In the heat of a summer's eve, I fell in love with you...
- Laughter is the sun that drives winter from the human face.
- Love is the light of Christmas.
- Smell the honeysuckle in the warm spring breeze.
- Snowflakes are angel kisses. Pucker up!
- Softly has a new snow you drifted into my life.
- Spring's greatest joy beyond a doubt is when it brings the children out. - Edgar Guest
- The future lies before you like a path of driven snow. Be careful how you tread on it for every mark will show.
- The roses wind with laziness and such a gentle ease...
- The vineyards are blazing with the blush of fall, this harvest has been the most blessed of all. - LaTourelle
- 'Tis sweet perfume of lilacs scenting the morning breeze...
- Winter is an etching, spring a watercolor, summer an oil painting and autumn a mosaic of them all. - Horowitz
- Winter snow in the warmth of a fire fills my heart with love's desire.

Kissed by the breath of spring your heart pounding into my soul, we embrace the innocence of our youth and come together in passionate closeness as our hearts become of one accord in love.

The harvest moon is glowing
The air is crisp and clear
Autumn winds are blowing
It's my favorite time of year!
 – Jennifer Byerly

When autumn's wind begins to blow
The leaves play in the street
I marvel at the way they dance
And twirl around my feet!
 – Jennifer Byerly

Here's a special card for you
Your friendship is the reason
Fond thoughts for you are on my mind
No matter what the season!
 – Jennifer Byerly

When the autumn leaves start blowing
The leaves begin to race
The scarecrow guards the pumpkin patch
With his friendly face
The crispness of the cool fall air
Is evident at night
Don't forget the harvest moon
Glowing round and bright!
 – Jennifer Byerly

Thought is the blossom; language the bud; action the fruit behind it.
~ Ralph Waldo Emerson

The year's at the spring and the day's at the morn;
Morning's at seven; the hillside's dew-pearled;
The lark's on the wing; the snail's on the thorn;
God's in his heaven–all's right with the world!
 – Robert Browning

SECRET PAL

Love is kind, Love is true
Love is the friendship
Between me and you
Your Secret Pal
~ CC Milam

On Your Special Day
Thinking of You
You are in my thoughts today
and just a prayer away!
Your Secret Pal
- GG Milam

Dear Secret Pal,
It is hard to believe the time
is here for you to know.
As I think through the year,
where did the time go?
I have enjoyed each month
and the thoughts of you
praying the Lord would bless
in everything that you do
May He continue to lead you and guide
May He always keep you close by His side.
In His Love, Your Secret Pal
- GG Milam

May the Lord lead you and guide you
today and everyday and in every way!
Your Secret Pal

A Gift for You

Here is a gift I made just for you.
I think you are special in all that you do.
May you have a wonderful week
And find blessings in all that you seek.
– GG Milam

Dear Secret Santa,

You were just so very clever
A thoughtful, happy soul
Dear secret Santa thank you
For not giving lumps of coal!
Once you were revealed
I smiled to myself
Because you made a wonderful
Jolly sort of elf!
– Jennifer Byerly

To My Secret Pal

May the Lord watch over you and keep
You in all that you do throughout your day.
May He send His peace and comfort
And fill you with blessings in every way.
You're in my prayers today and always
Your Secret Pal
– GG Milam

I'm as clever as clever can be...
I bet you can't guess that this is from me!
This is fun. It is really neat.
To give you presents that are really sweet.
~ CC Milam

SPIRITUAL

◎ And he shall be like a tree planted by the rivers of water, that bringeth forth his fruit in his season; his leaf also shall not wither; and whatsoever he doeth shall prosper. - Psalm 1:3 KJV

◎ Begin to weave and God will give you the thread.

◎ Do your best and then, sleep in peace. God is awake.

◎ God has a purpose for me no one else can fulfill.

◎ How come you're always running around looking for God? He's not lost.

◎ I have discovered that when the Almighty wants me to do or not do a particular thing, He has a way of letting me know it. - Abraham Lincoln

◎ It's my business to do God's business and it's His business to take care of my business.

◎ Jesus said, "I am light of the world. Whoever follows me will never walk in darkness, but will have the light of life." - John 8:12 NIV

◎ Know that the Lord is God; it is He who has made us, and not we ourselves; we are His people, and the sheep of His pasture. - Psalm 100:3 NIV

◎ No matter what is happening in your life, know that God is waiting for you with open arms.

◎ Prayer: Don't bother to give God instructions, just report for duty.

◎ Sometimes when God says "no," it's because He has something better in store for you.

◎ What makes us special is the signature of God on our lives. - Max Lucado

◎ You will seek Me and find Me, when you seek Me with all your heart.

God asks that we serve as He calls us
In the place where He wants us to be
He asks that we faithfully follow
What our eyes don't allow us to see

God blesses our lives with our friendships
But his concern is more for the way
We show to the people we're meeting
As we travel life's path every day

God knows that the choices are many
But the answers are simple and sweet
If we stay in His word as we're living
He'll reward us the day that we meet

God knows that the way isn't easy
His son walked this earth as our proof
But He promised us no earthly roses
Just eternal life in His truth!
– Jennifer Byerly

All Scripture is God-breathed and is useful for
teaching, rebuking, correcting and training in
righteousness, so that the man of God may be
thoroughly equipped for every good work.
– II Timothy 3:16-17 NIV

The Lord

has a way of bringing us to the point where we must look up at Him, where we must seek Him with all of our heart and being. He loves us so and knows what is best for us. If only we would seek Him at the first of each day instead of at the fall of our trials. He is so faithful and forgiving. He loves like no other. We can always return to Him as a humble child and He will gently wipe away each tear.   – GG Milam

ST. PATRICK'S DAY

- ◉ Feelin' Green
- ◉ Leapin' Leprechauns
- ◉ May your right hand always be stretched out in friendship and never in want
- ◉ The Luck of the Irish—Happy St Patty's Day
- ◉ Top o' the morning

God and his angels close at hand,
Friends and family, their love impart,
And Irish blessings in your heart!

I'm looking over a four leaf clover
That I over-looked before.
One leaf is sunshine, the second is rain,
Third is the roses that grows in the lane.
No need explaining the one remaining
Is somebody I adore.

May there always be work for your hands to do,
May your purse always hold a coin or two.
May the sun always shine warm on your windowpane,
May a rainbow be certain to follow each rain.
May the hand of a friend always be near you,
And may God fill your heart with gladness to cheer you.

May your thoughts be as glad as the shamrocks.
May your heart be as light as a song.
May each day bring you bright happy hours,
That stay with you all year long.
For each petal on the shamrock
This brings a wish your way
Good health, good luck, and happiness
For today and every day.

STRESS

◎ A diamond is a chunk of coal that was made good under pressure. Hope your load is lifted soon.

◎ A grudge is a heavy thing to carry.

◎ But my God shall supply all your needs according to His riches in glory by Christ Jesus. - Philippians 4:19 KJV

◎ Be still and know that I am God. - Psalm 46:10 NIV

◎ Ever wait too long to start a project? Adds drama to your life doesn't it! Take it one day at a time and it will pass.

◎ For every minute you are angry with someone, you lose 60 seconds of happiness that you can never get back.

◎ I don't suffer from stress. I am a carrier.

◎ I know God will not give me anything I can't handle. I just wish that He didn't trust me so much. - Mother Teresa

◎ I read this article that said the typical symptoms of stress are eating too much, impulse buying, and driving too fast. Are they kidding? That is my idea of a perfect day.

◎ I'm a little stressed right now—just turn around and leave quietly and no one gets hurt. -Weaver

◎ If not for stress, I'd have no energy at all.

◎ I'm the MOMMY that's WHY!

◎ Stress is when you wake up screaming and you realize you haven't fallen asleep yet.

◎ The best way to forget all your troubles- wear tight shoes.

◎ To avoid stress at home-wear pearls and high heels-June Cleaver always looked great!

◎ We cannot change the direction of the wind... but we can adjust our sails.

◎ We never relax around here. Stress holds us together!

◎ When anxiety was great within me, your consolation brought joy to my soul. - Psalm 94:19 NIV

- When we put our cares in His hands, He puts His peace in our hearts. Cast your cares upon Him for He cares for you.
- You can only eat the elephant one bite at a time.
- You can't change the past, but you can ruin the present by worrying over the future.

I'm feeling rather sassy today
Nothing can frighten me!
Nothing is going to cause me stress
I'm as strong as I can be!!
No one is going to get me down
Or cause me to whimper and whine
You have to treat me with respect
I've earned it, it is mine!
I'm going to tackle all those tasks
That seem to overwhelm
There's a new woman steering this ship-
A toughie at the helm.
I'm-oh what is that awful sound?
That ringing in my ear?
Oh, it's my alarm clock going off
Time to wake up, I fear!!!
    – Thena Smith

The kids are fussy and
The hubby is grumpy
The beds aren't made
And the gravy is lumpy.
But my home is full
Of the ones I love best
So I ask you Lord
To bless this mess

The Lord is my light and my salvation; whom shall I fear? The Lord is stronghold of my life of whom shall be afraid? ~ Psalm 27:1 NIV

SUPPORT

A smile is cheer to you and me
The cost is nothing-it's given free
It comforts the weary-gladdens the sad
Consoles those in trouble-good or bad
To rich and poor-beggar or thief
It's free to all of any belief
A natural gesture of young and old
Cheers on the faint-disarms the bold
Unlike most blessings for which we pray
It's one thing we keep when we give it a way.

Trust in the Lord with all your heart and lean not on your own understanding. In all your ways acknowledge Him and He will make your paths straight. - Proverbs 3:5-6 NIV

But they that wait upon the Lord shall renew their strengths, they shall mount up with wings of eagles. They shall run and not be weary and they shall walk and not be faint. - Isaiah 40:31 KJV

I can do all things through Christ who strengthens me.
~ Philippians 4:13 NIV

God is our refuge and strength, A very present help in trouble.
- Psalm 46:1 KJV

So do not fear; for I am with you, do not be dismayed, for I am your God; I will strengthen you, and help you: I will uphold you with my righteous right hand. - Isaiah 41:10

Because He Lives, I can face tomorrow!

Believe in the sun when it is not shining
Believe in love even when you are alone.
Believe in God when He is silent.

SYMPaThy

- Don't let your grief be measured by her worth for then your sorrow has no end. – Shakespeare

- For some moments in life there are no words. – Willy Wonka

- I didn't invent the rainy day, I just carry the best umbrella. Let me help with the storm.

- I will shield you from the storm says the Lord and calm the wildest sea. Reach out your heart and follow me.

- I'll be a friend to see you through the night, arms to hold you ever so tight, a candle always burning bright and love that wants to make everything right. – LaTourelle

- In those moments of sorrow, look up–for your Father is weeping with you. Call to His name and His heart will comfort you. – LaTourelle

- May the concern and sympathy of those who care help you through this difficult time.

- May the Lord comfort your heart as only He can do.

- One must learn to be still in the midst of turmoil to feel the unmistakable presence of strength.

- Thinking of you today and lifting you up in prayer.

- Trust in the Lord with all your heart and lean not on your own understanding. – Proverbs 3:5 NIV

- When someone you love becomes a memory...The memory becomes a treasure.

- Wishing we could be by your side at this time, our deepest sympathy.

- Wishing you a day of special moments in this time of sorrow and treasured memories to lift you up.

- Wishing you hope in the midst of sorrow, comfort in the midst of pain.

- With heartfelt sympathy and kindest thoughts to you, in your sorrow.

What though the radiance,
Which was once so bright,
Be now forever taken from my sight,
Though nothing can bring back the hour
Of my splendor in the grass,
Of glory in the flowers:
We will grieve not, rather find
Strength in what remains behind.
– Wordsworth

Even if you're hurting today,
If you look forward to tomorrow,
For there's a very thin line
Between happiness and sorrow.

Let me be your hope when life seems desperate
Let me be your laughter crying through the tears
Let me be the touch that will lift your spirits
Let me be the heart beating strong for you
Let me be your strength when you're feeling weak
Let me be everything to you
– LaTourelle

Child

Although I haven't always
Had the words to give to you
To offer up some comfort
I hope you know it's true
Whenever we're together
Or whether we're apart
Thoughts and prayers for you
Dwell inside my heart
– Jennifer Byerly

Nestled in God's Arms

The Lord loves little ones
And keeps them safe and warm
In a special place in Heaven
Nestled in His arms.
The Lord placed the tiny babes
To grow in a mother's womb
And if He calls them home before their birth
He must have them a special room.
I have not yet seen Heaven
But I know our God above
Will take special care of tiny ones
And surround them with His love.
So do not fret or mourn
For the tiny soul set free
But look forward to a reunion
That will last eternally.
– Thena Smith

With Sympathy For Your Loss

When your dear child is suddenly gone.
Leaving you here to try and carry on.
To grieve in silence or scream out loud.
To say harsh words or to just be proud
Of her courageous battle to the end.
Knowing that you were her best friend,
much more than Mommy to this little girl.
You did everything to brighten her world.
She finally had to let go of your hand
To start her journey to a Heavenly land.
Tears may run in rivulets down your cheeks.
Sobbing in grief is not considered weak.
It helps with coping for the young and old.
A healing balm for the grieving soul.
– Lottie Ann Knox

From Grandparent

This picture is quite special
It's one of you and me
I held you up while smiling
For all the world to see
My precious little grandson
One day I'll get the chance
To tell you how I love you
In heaven when we dance
But 'til that day arrives
I'll watch you all your days
As I sit amongst the angels
Blowing kisses down your way!
– Jennifer Byerly

Loved One

May the memories you have of your loved one
Sustain you like no memory hath
May you find your way out of sorrow
As you walk this difficult path!
– Jennifer Byerly

I have no words to express my sorrow,
Only my love and the tears I will shed tomorrow.
Family is precious and dear to me and
To lose one breaks my heart you see.
For I know he is in a better place,
And he is seeing Jesus face to face.
So where do we go from here you might say,
I think we should first stop and take time to pray.
And read our Bibles to see what He has told.
And to live life everyday as Jesus showed.
– by August Jones for his Uncle Chester Jones 2003

Springtime in Heaven

Our Gertrude has made her journey home
And left us here to reminisce
About all of the sweet memories of her
And speak of those things that we shall miss.

She fills such a special place in our hearts
And we loved her more than words can say
Such precious memories rest in our hearts
And it will never go away.

But as much as we love her
And difficult as this may seem
We know that Heaven must be lovely
Especially in the Spring.

We know that God looks down on us
And sees our hurting hearts today
But our Gertrude is a lovely flower
In His Heavenly bouquet.

We know that if Gertrude can see us now
She is smiling at us in her sweet way
And would have us to remember her with love
But not weep that she has gone away.

She would have us feel the breeze
That lingers on our face
And think of it as a gentle kiss
And to remember her embrace.

The Springtime she would have us enjoy
And not cling to grief and sadness
For she had a wonderful life
And lived each day with gladness.

So join with us today in reliving
Those most precious of memories
And rejoice with us in the life we celebrate
And we're sure Gertrude will be pleased.

– by Thena Smith in memory of Gertrude Murial Shaw on March 21st, 2004

May God hold you in the palm
Of His hand. May the stumbling
Blocks along your way be
Stepping stones for you today.
I am here to lift you up
To brighten all your days
My arms will gladly hold you
And wipe your tears away
– LaTourelle

May the memories of your loved one bring comfort
As you walk this difficult path
May the joy of remembering good times
Sustain you like no memory hath
May you feel their presence surround you
As it holds you up through the years
May you find life worthwhile,
When one day you can smile
As you're facing the pain through your tears
– Jennifer Byerly

Dear Sister-in-Law to Be,

I'm certain that it was no accident
When you entered my dear brother's life
And I know that God will be smiling
At the moment you become his sweet wife
If by chance you should see my eyes glisten
On the day that you marry my brother
Please know that it comes from the blessing
Of knowing you're meant for each other
I believe that you love him so deeply
Still there's something I must say to you
Please honor and cherish him always
Because I love and adore him too!
As I extend a personal welcome
To our family please know that it's true
I look forward to calling you "sister"
And the chance to be good friends with you!
– Jennifer Byerly

Take Time To Grieve

Take time to grieve
And yes, to weep
But cherish sweet memories
For those you will keep

Do not forget
Though it now makes you sad
For someday remembering
Will again make you glad.

We know that sorrow
Never entirely goes away
But the burden will grow lighter
And you live from day to day.

Rejoice in the time
That you had to love
And look forward to reunion someday
In Heaven above.

For God knows every heartache
And He sees every tear
And the one that you love so much
The Father also holds dear.
– Thena Smith

Shared sorrow is sorrow halved.

May your memories bring you comfort
As you walk this difficult path
May the joy your loved one brought you
Sustain you like no memory hath
May you feel his presence surround you
And hold you up through the years
May a smile find you
And help to dry your tears
– Jennifer Byerly

Parent

They say that time heals all things
We wonder if that's true
It's been a year yet we know
Our tears aren't nearly through
We find small bits of comfort
In daily thoughts of dad
Memories that make moments
At times a bit less sad
And then there are the times when
We're sure we hear his voice
Through an earthly message
And then our hearts rejoice
We believe our father
Sends these messages of hope
On days when we feel we need
His love to help us cope
We don't know what tomorrow
Will bring, so come what may
But we'll always know our father
Is watching us each day!
    – Jennifer Byerly

Spouse

Sometimes it seems like yesterday
But it's been many years
The day two special people vowed
To share their joy and tears
As man and wife they shared their life,
And always they did cling
Until the day one went away
Upon an angel's wing
But love is strong and now the song
On which one heart depends
Is keeping beat with memories
Sweet until they meet again
    – Jennifer Byerly

Teacher's Day

- A teacher affects eternity; he can never tell.
- Education is not the filling of a bucket but the lighting of a fire. – W.B. Yeats
- I like a teacher who gives you something to take home to think about besides homework.
- In the service of the Lord, it is not where you serve, but how. – J. Reuben Clark, Jr.
- Often, when I read a book, I stop and thank my teacher. That is, I used to, until she got an unlisted number.
- Some people come into our lives and quickly go... Others stay and leave footprints on our hearts.
- Teacher's Task: to take a lot of hot wires and make sure that they are grounded.
- Teachers are a kids best friend.
- Teachers are in a class all their own.
- Teachers can't live on apples alone.
- Teachers make kids count.
- Teachers Rule!
- Thank you for your lasting impression on my life.
- Thanks for being such a wonderful teacher to my child and making a difference to her.
- Thanks for teaching me to love learning and others.
- You've been more than a teacher to me–You've been a friend. Happy Teacher's Day

Teachers are the tenders
In the gardens of their care
That keep a classroom happy
With children blooming there!
~ Jennifer Byerly

Thank You

For teaching children lessons,
To help them as they grow,
Let this gift remind you,
You're the best teacher we know!

Teachers are so special

To every girl and boy
They fill our minds with knowledge
And making learning such a joy

You are a very special teacher
Always giving and sharing
Teaching us to love learning
And showing us love by caring

You're the best!

Teachers are like angels
Watching out for you
Giving you direction
In what you say and do
They hover near while teaching
And help you learn and grow
They're amongst my favorite people
And such a joy to know!
— Jennifer Byerly

I chose this special present because I wanted you to know,
That I'm grateful for your hard work in helping me to grow.
For your constant understanding and for always being there,
To tell me I can do it and to show me that you care!

A teacher is someone who's caring
A teacher is someone who's kind
A teacher is someone with knowledge
To fill up a young person's mind

They work when the hour is early
They work when the hour is late
They often work right through their lunchtime
Grading papers on their coffee break

For it takes a special commitment
To do all the things that they do
We're proud of all of our teachers
And grateful for each one of you!
– Jennifer Byerly

Reading, writing, 'rithmetic
Crayons, pencils, books
Wednesday planning, scoring guides
And all the time they took
Meetings, testing, speeches, grades
No time for coffee breaks
Late start when the children are
So much more awake!

Conference, phone calls, written notes
Planning out your day
Lunchtime with your peers and friends
A time to get away
Recess duty, music class, assemblies in the gym
Mounds and mounds of paper work
Often lacking R.E.M.

Of all the jobs that teachers have
There's none that can replace
Caring for and teaching each
Eager, learning face!
– Jennifer Byerly

We recognize the hard work
It takes for you to teach
The schooling and credentials
Each teacher has to reach

Yet the things of highest value
And importance that you hold
Aren't framed on any paper
They're worth much more than gold

Not found in any textbook
They're not from any class
And once you have attained them
The value lasts and lasts

It's the character you're holding
When every day is through
The life skills that you carry
That credit all of you

So thank you for committing
To be the very best
You've earned the highest marks
On the most important test!
    - Jennifer Byerly

Deep within a teacher's heart
A mother's love resides
She loves and nurtures children
And watches them with pride
Her job is one that goes beyond
Their academic best
Managing their daily needs
Can put her to the test
She listens to their problems
And celebrates their joy
Best of all her heart has room
For every girl and boy
    - Jennifer Byerly

Thank You

- And whatever you do, whether in word or deed, do it all in the name of the Lord Jesus, giving thanks to God the Father through him. - Colossians 3:17 NIV

- Be joyful always; pray continually; give thanks in all circumstances, for this is God's will for you in Christ Jesus. - I Thessalonians 5:16-18 NIV

- Being in your prayers is the best place to be. Thanks!

- Blessed are those that can give without remembering and receive without forgetting.

- Contentment is not the fulfillment of what you want, but the realization of how much you already have.

- Friends like you are wonderful.

- How far that little candle throws his beams! So shines a good deed in a weary world. - William Shakespeare

- It is with great pleasure we welcome you.

- Just a little thanks for your giant blessing.

- Let the peace of Christ rule in your hearts, since as members of one body you were called to peace. And be thankful. - Colossians 3:15 NIV

- Let us be grateful to people who make us happy; they are the charming gardeners who make our souls blossom. - M. Proust

- May someone be as kind to you as you were to me. Thank you so much!

- No duty is more urgent than that of returning thanks. From the bottom of my heart you have touched my life. Thank you so much for everything.

- Thank you for always listening to me with your heart.

- Thank you for being the kind of friend I can count on! I really appreciate you!

- Thank you for being you!

- ◉ Thank you for believing in what I was becoming even before it was clear to see from a distance.
- ◉ Thank you for brightening up my day.
- ◉ Thank you for opening so many doors, then seeing me through them!
- ◉ Thank you for teaching my heart to dance with the stars.
- ◉ Thank you for the helpful gift. I put it to use right away!
- ◉ Thank you for the housewarming gift. It was quite toasty!
- ◉ Thank you for the wonderful gift! You shouldn't have!
- ◉ Thank you for your kindest expression of concern for me.
- ◉ Thank you for your thoughtfulness in thinking of me at this time in my life.
- ◉ Thank you for your wonderful expression of love.
- ◉ Thank you Lord, for my family.
- ◉ Thank you. You're so sweet from the top of your head to the bottom of your feet. - CC Milam
- ◉ Thanks for thinking of me.
- ◉ Thanks for your business.
- ◉ Thanks so much for the hospitality.
- ◉ The baby gift is a wonderful expression of love. Thank you.
- ◉ We are grateful for the gift and making our house a home.
- ◉ What would I do without you?? You help to keep my eyes on the road and my path straight. Many Thanks!
- ◉ With deep appreciation
- ◉ With special thanks and much appreciation for your friendship, your business and the opportunity to serve you. You are kind, you are thoughtful, you are appreciated!
- ◉ You are so kind and so considerate. Thanks a million!
- ◉ You're so thoughtful. Thank you for your kindness.
- ◉ You've done so many nice things for me I don't know. where to start-Eeny meeney-thanks!

How does one thank you
For all the things you do?
In the dictionary under generosity
Should be a photo of you!

How does one thank you
For all the things you do?
I do not know what we would have done
Had it not been for you!

How do we express our feelings
For the things you did for us
Never expecting gratitude or praise
And never wanting a fuss?

All I can do is say "Thank You"
And hope that the meaning is clear
That is a deep heart felt thanks
And pray that it's depth your heart can hear!
- Thena Smith

Thanks for celebrating
My special day with me
You helped create a special
Batch of memories
- Jennifer Byerly

In appreciation of your hospitality, I have prepared a short
heartfelt speech to express my sincere gratitude.
Here it is... Thanks!

For all the ways you've cared for me,
For all the love you've shared with me,
For always being there with me,
Thank you!

This little book can only begin
To thank you for all you do
And most of all to express
Just how grateful we are for you!
– Thena Smith

Angel wings and diamond rings
Are lovely things indeed
I don't care, they don't compare
When someone's kind to me!

The nicest things are often things
That none of us can touch
That's why I'm sending you this card
To thank you very much
– Jennifer Byerly

*May it brighten your day in some small
Way to know how much I care.
Thank you for your friendship*

Gratitude is the heart's memory
In our daily work day world
Sometimes it's hard to impart
All the love and gratitude
That's in our heart.
Sometimes there seems to be
No words to say
That you enrich our lives
And bless our day.
But with this little book
Let us try to show you
Just how we really feel
As our feelings of friendship
and love we reveal.

Thanksgiving

The Turkey is a funny bird
His head goes wobble wobble,
but all that he can ever say,
is Gobble, Gobble, Gobble.

*Ain't nothing like Mama's holiday
cookin' to make a body warm*

The vineyards are blazing with the blush of fall,
This harvest has been the most blessed of all
Forever on Thanksgiving Day the heart
Will find the pathway home.
– Roger North

*Thanksgiving is a time to give thanks to the Lord
for family, friends, health, and wealth.*

For each new morning with its light,
For rest and shelter of the night,
For health and food, for love and friends,
For everything Thy goodness sends.
– Ralph Waldo Emerson

Do not get tired of doing what is good. Don't get
Discouraged and give up, for we will reap a
harvest of blessing at the appropriate time.
– Book of Galatians

Let us give thanks to the Lord up above, Who blesses us
each day with His grace and love. Thank you, Lord, for
each new day you bring. We lift up our voice and with
praises we sing. Glory, honor, and praises to you! For all the
blessings you give, we thank you.   – Linda LaTourelle

I'm sending you this message
And your friendship is the reason
In hopes that you will join me
And be thankful for this season!
– Jennifer Byerly

Stuffed Like a Turkey!
Turkey, gravy, cranberry
Pumpkin pie, whipped cream
Mashed potatoes, hot fresh rolls
Cold cider, fresh green beans
Olives, carrots, jello salad
Candied Yams so sweet
I'm stuffed up like a turkey
From my head down to my feet!
– Jennifer Byerly

The turkey is on the table
Roasted a golden brown,
There's stuffing, potatoes and gravy
And cider to wash it down.
There's pumpkin pie and apple
Maybe a chocolate one too,
Friends and family are gathered
For all this, Father, we thank you.
– Sharon Ezzell

The table is laden with bountiful food
Friends and family are gathered around,
We are safe and warm, and together
What better blessings than these could be found.
– Sharon Ezzell

A bounty of good wishes. A harvest full of love.
A horn-a-plenty filled with lots of
blessings from above! ~ Jennifer Byerly

A Thanksgiving Blessing

May you be uplifted by the cool, crisp autumn air
May your heart be warmed by special moments
Filled with special joys to share...
May your soul be touched by God's wonder
At the treasures to be found as you celebrate
Thanksgiving and His beauty all around.

Scripture on Thankfulness

As long as the earth endures, seedtime and harvest, cold and heat, summer and winter, day and night will never cease. – Genesis 8:22 NIV

Be joyful always; pray continually; give thanks in all circumstances, for this is God's will for you in Christ Jesus. – Thessalonians 5:16-18 NIV

Celebrate the Feast of Harvest with the firstfruits of the crops you sow in your field. Celebrate the Feast of Ingathering at the end of the year, when you gather in your crops from the field. – Exodus 23:16 NIV

Enter his gates with thanksgiving and his courts with praise; give thanks to him and praise his name. – Psalm 100:4 NIV

Give thanks to the LORD, for he is good; his love endures forever. – I Chronicles 16:34 NIV

I always thank God for you because of his grace given you in Christ Jesus. – I Corinthians 1:4 NIV

I will praise God's name in song and glorify him with thanksgiving. – Psalm 69:30 NIV

Then the land will yield its harvest, and God, our God, will bless us. – Psalm 67:6 NIV

When he was at the table with them, he took bread, gave thanks, broke it and began to give it to them. – Luke 24:30 NIV

THINKING OF YOU

This is what I wish for you–
joyous times beyond compare
someone who is always there
comfort when days are blue
hugs to always shelter you
peace like a dove
faith from above summer
sunsets on a winter's night
birds that sing on winged flight
rainbows after every storm
sunny days to keep you warm
kisses from lips so sweet
twinkling toes and dancing feet
all of this and so much more
is sent with love to the one I adore
– LaTourelle

As deep as the ocean
As huge as the sky
You are the
Apple of my eye
~ CC Milam

Our lives are sewn together with threads of loving care.
Each day we're blessed with opportunities to share.
And so I take this moment to send some thoughts your way,
Wrapped in love and goodness as I think of you and pray.
– LaTourelle

Thinking of you on this happy day
Thinking of you in a special way
Thinking of you and letting you know
I'm thinking of you and loving you so.
– GG Milam

Sometimes we hit a pothole
As we travel down life's road
The way gets rather bumpy
And we bear a weighty load
Always keep your faith
No matter what you do
Because the path with Jesus
Will be smoother then for you!
– Jennifer Byerly

Did you know?
Did you know that I wanted to see you smile?
Did you know I 'd walk that extra mile?
Did you know there is only one love so true?
Did you know that person is simply you?
~ LaTourelle

One hour with thee! When sun is set,
Oh, what can teach me to forget
The thankless labors of the day:
The hopes, the wishes, flung away;
The increasing wants, and lessening gains,
The master's pride, who scorns my pains?
One hour with thee.
– Sir Walter Scott

I thank my God every time I remember you.
~ Philippians 1:3 NIV

VALENTINE'S DAY

- Be still my heart and be mine.
- Bee Mine
- Candy Kisses and Champagne Wishes...
- Cupid, draw back your arrow straight to my lover's heart.
- Give me what you alone can give–A kiss to build a dream.
- Hugs and Kisses
- I love you for sentimental reasons.
- If I could wrap love in a ribbon, it would be my gift to you.
- Love doesn't make the world go 'round. Love is what makes the ride worthwhile. – Franklin P. Jones
- Love Bug
- Love Letters
- My Funny Valentine
- My Heart's Desire
- SWAK and a hug, too!
- The sweetest joy, the wildest woe is love.
- To love is to believe... to hope... to know...
- True Love
- Two souls with but a single thought. Two hearts that beat as one. – Bellinghausen
- Two-lips just for you
- When a Man Loves a Woman
- Whosoever loves, believes the impossible.
- Will You Be My Valentine?
- You are what happened when I wished upon a star.
- You hold the Key to My Heart.
- You must remember this, a kiss is still a kiss...
- You're all I need my love, My Valentine.

You've always been that special
Darling I adore
Your smiles and your laughter
Warm me to the core
Of this I know I'll always
Count on all my days
Sweetheart you are someone
Who sets my heart ablaze!
– Jennifer Byerly

These are my gifts for you
Three little words that
Ring so sweet to my ears
Simply put ~ I Love You

You are as fair and sweet and tender,
Dear brown-eyed little sweetheart mine,
As when, a callow youth and slender,
I asked to be your Valentine.

So take, dear love, this little token,
And if there speaks in any line
The sentiment I'd fain have spoken,
Say, will you kiss your Valentine?

I swear to thee by Cupid's strongest bow,
By his best arrow with the golden head,
By the simplicity of Venus' doves,
By that which knitteth souls and prospers loves,
By all the vows that ever men have broke
(In number more than ever women spoke).
– William Shakespeare

VETERAN'S DAY

In Flanders Fields

In Flanders field the poppies blow
Between the crosses, row on row,
That mark our place; and in the sky
The larks, still bravely singing, fly
Scarce heard amid the guns below.
We are the Dead. Short days ago
We lived, felt dawn, saw sunset glow,
Loved and were loved, and now we lie
In Flanders fields.

Take up our quarrel with the foe:
To you from failing hands we throw
The torch; be yours to hold it high.
If ye break with us who die
We shall not sleep, though poppies grow
In Flanders fields.
- Major John McCrae, May 1915

*Thank you for taking a stand
and fighting for
Our Country ~ Our freedom*

With gratitude and respect
I'm sending this card your way.
Words can not express the feelings
And the thanks for the sacrifice you
Made for your country and your family.
- GG Milam

*We honor you
Men of Red, White & Blue*

WEDDINGS

◎ A Celebration of Love

◎ A kiss to build a dream on.

◎ A match made in heaven.

◎ All my love, all my life... Always & Forever.

◎ And the fairy tale begins...

◎ And the two shall be called One

◎ And they will live happily ever after...

◎ As I give you my hand to hold, I give you my heart to keep.

◎ Be one in heart and always in mind.

◎ Best wishes for a long and happy marriage

◎ Can you feel the love tonight?

◎ Congratulations, on this, your special day.

◎ Could I have this dance?

◎ Dance me to the end of love

◎ For the Bride and Groom—May all the love two hearts can hold be yours through a wonderful life together.

◎ For this cause shall a man leave father and mother, and shall cleave unto his wife, and they shall become one flesh. - Matthew 19:5 KJV

◎ From long ago and far away, love brought to our wedding day!

◎ Happiness is marrying your best friend

◎ Happy Wedding Day

◎ Have I told you lately that I Love You?

◎ He Loves Me, He Loves Me Not, He Loves Me!

◎ He who finds a wife finds a good thing, and obtains favor from the Lord. - Proverbs 18:22 KJV

◎ How sweet it is to be loved by you. - Eddie Holland

◎ I love thee with the breath, smiles, tears of all my life!

- I wanna grow old with you.
- If ever two were one, then surely we. If ever man were loved by wife, then thee. – Anne Bradstreet
- If I know what love is, it is because of you.
- In all you dream and in all you do, may the love you share bring joy to you
- Love for time and eternity
- Love is patient; love is kind; love never ends.
- Love lives beyond the tomb, the earth, which fades like dew. I love the fond, the faithful, and the true.
- Marriage began in a garden
- Married couples who love each other tell each other a thousand things without talking. – Chinese Proverb
- May the Lord richly bless you today and always
- May the wings of angels carry you forever with this moment of wedded bliss always in your heart.
- May this day and always be filled with love and joy.
- Sharing joy with you today
- The Lord has brought you to this day for always.
- To the Bride and Groom
- To the Mr. & Mrs.
- Tonight is a celebration of you!
- Two hearts as one
- Two hearts... Two souls... One love... Forever
- What therefore God has joined together, let no man put asunder. – Mark 10:9 KJV
- When you meet someone who can cook and do housework, don't hesitate a minute—marry him!!
- Wrapped in Love with you
- With all that I am and all that I have and all that I hope to be, I will honor you with my life forever.

You are the mother I received
The day I wed your son.
And I just want to thank you, Mum
For all the things you've done.

You've given me a gracious man
With whom I share my life.
You are his loving mother and
I his lucky wife.

You used to pat his little head,
And now I hold his hand.
You raised in love a little boy
And gave to me a man.

For where your treasure is,
there will your heart be also.
~ Matthew 6:21 NIV

Woman was created from the rib of man,
not from his head to be above him,
nor his feet to be walked upon,
But from his side to be equal,
near his arm to be protected and
close to his heart to be loved.

For hearing my thoughts, understanding
my dreams and being my best friend,
For filling my life with joy and
Loving me without end,
"I do."

From This Day Forward

The road is bright before us,
As hand in hand we start,
We'll travel on together,
One mind, one soul, one heart.

Irish Wedding Blessing

May God be with you and Bless you
May you see your children's children
May you be poor in misfortune and
Rich in Blessings and
May you know nothing but
Happiness from this day forward.

The Blessing of The Apaches

Now you will feel no rain,
For each of you will be shelter to the other.
Now you will feel no cold,
For each of you will be warmth to the other.
Now there is no more loneliness for you,
For each of you will be companion to the other.
Now you are two bodies,
But there is only one life before you.
Go now to your dwelling place,
To enter into the days of your togetherness.
And may your days be good and long upon the earth.

To keep your marriage brimming,
With love in the wedding cup,
Whenever you're wrong, admit it;
Whenever you're right, shut up.
~ Ogden Nash

Dear Son,

I remember when you were a baby
It was love at first sight from the start
Each moment will live their forever
Taking residence up in my heart

Yes, the memories are etched there forever
Where I'll cherish them all of my life
As I've watched you grow into manhood
And now you'll soon take a wife

Overwhelmed by the joy I am feeling
And the love that I feel for you son
I'm so proud of the choices you're making
And the man that I've watched you become
- Jennifer Byerly

Dear Daughter,

The job I held as your mother
Was a job I loved from the start
Each day was like a new chapter
In a book that I store in my heart

The memories are etched there forever
Where I'll cherish them all of my life
As I watch you with joy my daughter
Take on the role of a wife

Overwhelmed by the pride I am feeling
It's important that you understand
I am proud of the life you are choosing
And I'll support you wherever I can!

Please know that my role as your mother
May be changing though it will not end
Because you're not just my daughter
I also see you as my friend!
- Jennifer Byerly

A White Rose

The red rose whispers of passion,
And the white rose breathes of love;
O the red rose is a falcon,
And the white rose is a dove.
But I send you a cream-white rosebud
With a flush on its petal tips;
For the love that is purest and sweetest
Has a kiss of desire on the lips.
– John Boyle O'Reilly

True Love

True love is a sacred flame
That burns eternally,
And none can dim its special glow
Or change its destiny.
True love speaks in tender tones
And hears with gentle ear,
True love gives with open heart
And true love conquers fear.
True love makes no harsh demands
It neither rules nor binds,
And true love holds with gentle hands
The hearts that it entwines.
Love Lives
– John Clare

I give you my love, more precious than money,
I give you myself before preaching or law:
Will you give me yourself?
Will you come travel with me?
Shall we stick by each other as long as we live?
~ Walt Whitman

Love's Philosophy

The Fountains mingle with the River and the Rivers with the Ocean, the winds of Heaven mix forever with a sweet emotion; Nothing in the world is single; All things by a law divine in one spirit meet and mingle. Why not I with thine? –see the mountains kiss high Heaven and the waves clasp one another; No sister-flower would be forgiven if it disdained its brother, and the sunlight clasps the earth and the moonbeams kiss the sea: What is all this sweet work worth if thou kiss not me?

- Percy Bysshe Shelley

Blessing for a Marriage

May your marriage bring you all the exquisite excitements a marriage should bring, and may life grant you also patience, tolerance, and understanding. May you always need one another–not so much to fill your emptiness as to help you know your fullness. A mountain needs a valley to be complete; the valley does not make the mountain less, but more; and the valley is more a valley because it has a mountain towering over it. So let it be with you and you. May you need one another, but not out of weakness. May you want one another, but not out of lack. May you entice one another, but not compel one another. May you succeed in all important ways with one another, and not fail in the little graces. May you look for things to praise, often say, "I love you!" and take no notice of small faults. If you have quarrels that push you apart, may both of you hope to have good sense enough to take the first step back. May you enter into the mystery which is the awareness of one another's presence–no more physical than spiritual, warm and near when you are side by side, and warm and near when you are in separate rooms or even distant cities. May you have happiness, and may you find it making one another happy. May you have love, and may you find it loving one another!

- James Dillet Freeman

Sonnet 18

Shall I compare thee to a summer's day?
Thou art more lovely and more temperate:
Rough winds do shake the darling buds of May,
And summer's lease hath all too short a date:
Sometime too hot the eye of heaven shines,
And often is his gold complexion dimm'd:
And every fair from fair sometime declines,
By chance, or nature's changing course untrimm'd:
But thy eternal summer shall not fade,
Nor lose possession of that fair thou ow'st;
Nor shall Death brag thou wander'st in his shade,
When in eternal lines to time thou grow'st:
So long as man can breathe, or eyes can see,
So long lives this, and this gives life to thee.
- William Shakespeare

When I fall in love, It will be forever.
When I give my heart, It will be completely
~ Edward Heyman

Come Live with Me and Be My Love

Come live with me and be my love, and we will all the
pleasures prove that valleys, groves, hills and fields, woods, or
steepy mountain yields. And we will sit upon the rocks, seeing
the shepherds feed their flocks, by shallow rivers to whose falls
melodious birds sing madrigals. And I will make thee beds of
roses and a thousand fragrant poises, a cap of flowers, and a
kirtle embroidered all with leaves of myrtle; A gown made of
finest wool which from our pretty lambs we pull; Fair lined
slippers for the cold, with buckles of the purest gold; A belt of
straw and ivy buds, with coral clasps and amber studs: And if
these pleasures may the move, come live with me, and be my
love. The shepherds' swains shall dance and sing for thy delight
each May morning: If these delights thy mind may move, then
live with me and be my love.   - Christopher Marlowe

This Day I Married My Best Friend

This day I married my best friend
...the one I laugh with as we share life's wondrous zest,
As we find new enjoyments and experience all that's best.
...the one I live for because the world seems brighter
As our happy times are better and our burdens feel much lighter.
...the one I love with every fiber of my soul.
We used to feel vaguely incomplete, now together we are whole.

Why Marriage?

Because to the depths of me, I long to love one person,
With all my heart, my soul, my mind, my body...
Because I need a forever friend to trust with the intimacies of me,
Who won't hold them against me,
Who loves me when I'm unlikable,
Who sees the small child in me, and
Who looks for the divine potential of me...
Because I need to cuddle in the warmth of the night
With someone who thanks God for me,
With someone I feel blessed to hold...
Because marriage means opportunity
To grow in love, in friendship...
Because marriage is a discipline
To be added to a list of achievements...
Because marriages do not fail, people fail
When they enter into marriage
Expecting another to make them whole...
Because, knowing this,
I promise myself to take full responsibility
For my spiritual, mental and physical wholeness
I create me, I take half of the responsibility for my marriage
Together we create our marriage...
Because of this understanding
The possibilities are limitless.

Love lives in sleep,
The happiness of healthy dreams
Eve's dews may weep,
But love delightful seems.
'Tis heard in Spring
When light and sunbeams, warm and kind,
On angels' wing
Bring love and music to the mind,
And where is voice,
So young, so beautiful and sweet
As nature's choice,
Where Spring and lovers meet?
Love lives beyond
The tomb, the earth, the flowers, and dew.
I love the fond,
The faithful, young and true.

A Good Wedding Cake

4 lb of love.
1 lb butter of youth.
1/2 lb of good looks.
1 lb sweet temper.
1 lb of blindness for faults.
1 lb of self-forgetfulness.
1 lb of pounded wit.
1 lb of good humor.
2 tablespoons of sweet argument.
1 pint of rippling laughter.
1 wine glass of common sense.
1 oz modesty.

Put in the love, good looks and sweet temper into a well furnished house. Beat the butter of youth to a cream, and mix well together with the blindness of faults. Stir the pounded wit and good humor into the sweet argument, then add the rippling laughter and common sense. Work the whole together until everything is well mixed, and bake gently forever.

WiSDoM

- A diamond is a piece of coal that finished what it started.
- Always do right. This will amaze most people, and astonish the rest. - Mark Twain
- Deal with the fault of others as gently as your own.
- Doing the best at this moment puts you in the best place for the next moment.
- Dreams come true, without that possibility, nature would not invite us to have them. - John Updike
- Education is what you get from reading the fine print. Experience is what you get from not reading it.
- Every good thought you think is contributing its share to the ultimate result of your life.
- Happiness is a direction, not a place. - Syndey J. Harris
- He is happiest who finds peace in his home.
- It is not the pursuit of happiness that we find fulfillment, it is the happiness of pursuit. - Denis Waitley
- Life happens while you are making plans.
- Life is like a mirror, we get the best results when we smile at it.
- Oh, the places you'll go, oh, the things you'll see. - Dr. Seuss
- The first half of our lives are ruined by our parents, and the second half by our children. - Clarence Darrow
- The happiest moments of my life have been the few which I have passed at home in the bosom of my family. - T. Jefferson
- The fear of the Lord is the beginning of knowledge. - Proverbs 1:7 NIV
- What lies behind us, and what lies before us are tiny matters compared to what lies within us. - Emerson
- What matters is what you do with what you already have.
- Your life is made up of years that mean nothing; moments that mean it all!

Life is a song—sing it.
Life is a game—play it.
Life is a challenge—meet it.
Life is a dream—realize it.
Life is a sacrifice—offer it.
Life is love—enjoy it.

I wish I were wise
And had profound things to say
That would help mankind
And my world someway.

I wish I knew exactly
The right thing to say
To lift someone's spirit
Or brighten their day.

But wishing won't make
All of my wishes come true
But One wish of mine did
When I wished for you.
– Thena Smith

Listen, my son, to your father's instruction
And do not forsake your mother's teaching.
They will be a garland to grace your head
And a chain to adorn your neck.
– Proverbs 1:8-9 NIV

Instruct a wise man and he will be wiser still;
Teach a righteous man and he will add to his learning.
The fear of the Lord is the beginning of wisdom
And knowledge of the Holy One is understanding.
For through me your days will be many,
And years will be added to your life.
If you are wise, your wisdom will reward you.
– Proverbs 9:9-12 NIV

When we do the best that we can, we never know what miracle is wrought in our life, or in the life of another.   – Helen Keller

If you look at what you have in life, you'll always have more. If you look at what you don't have in life, you'll never have enough.   – Oprah Winfrey

We are all artists gently guided by our Master's hand, painting a vision called life The blending of colors like joy, sorrow, wisdom and love inspire us to create a magnificent masterpiece of self. – Linda LaTourelle

The person who tries to live alone will not succeed as a human being. His heart withers if it does not answer another heart. His mind shrinks away if he hears only the echoes of his own thoughts and finds no other inspiration.

The Purpose of Life is a Life of Purpose

To laugh is to risk appearing a fool, To weep is to risk appearing sentimental. To reach out to another is to risk involvement, To expose feelings is to risk exposing your true self. To place your ideas and dreams before a crowd is to risk their loss. To love is to risk not being loved in return, To live is to risk dying, To hope is to risk despair, To try is to risk failure. But risks must be taken because the greatest hazard in life is to risk nothing. The person who risks nothing, does nothing, has nothing, is nothing. He may avoid suffering and sorrow, but he cannot learn, feel, change, grow or live. Chained by his servitude he is a slave who has forfeited all freedom. Only a person who risks is free.

Imagination is the SOUL within
~ LaTourelle

Wish You Were Here

- Absence makes my heart ache... Missing you
- Being here is just no fun without you.
- Cozy by the fire, snuggled on the rug...Wishing you were here for me to kiss and hug
- I am here and you are there...This really does seem unfair
- I'm here and you are not... Nanna Nanna
- Loving the sights and wishing you were here to see the beauty of it all
- No miles of any measurement can separate your soul from mine. - Antonio Suave
- Such lovely sights I see but my heart is wish you were here with me
- Wish you were here or wish I were there or wish the two of us were together....anywhere! - Thena Smith
- Wish you were here... What can I say, your presence always makes for a very special day. - Thena Smith

Though miles and time separates us
The bond that we share in our hearts
Is a love that will keep us together
Even though we must now be apart!
- Jennifer Byerly

Sun and sand and daily fun
Places to go always on the run...
Getting up to start a brand new day
New things to see along the way...
Joy and laughter and immense delight
Made our time together so happy and bright!
Our vacation was wonderful and we felt blessed
But no matter where we visit, home is always best!!
- Thena Smith

Horizon

Look out into the horizon
What is it that you see?
A place where the sun
Melts into the trees
A place where the sky
Becomes the sea

A place for new beginnings
A place where it ends
It is a vast mountain
Snow-capped white

It is the day solely fading to night
It is boundless in dreams
No boundaries will you find
If you should follow it
You would surely travel forever...
- Teri Olund

This year on this day
Raise your face up to the skies
And feel my love reign down as
You slowly close your eyes!

Though an ocean separates us
We still share the same sky
The same sun shines upon us
The same moon on the rise

So tonight if you should want to
Please wish upon a star
And I'll be wishing with you
Across the miles far!
- Jennifer Byerly

Missing You...

WOMAN TO WOMAN

- A man's got to do what a man's got to do. A woman must do what he can't.
- A wise man once said, "I don't know. Go ask a woman."
- And you are telling me this because???
- And your point IS...
- Give a girl the right shoes and she can conquer the world.
- Goddess... formerly Princess
- I called in sick today... I broke a nail.
- I'm still hot. It just comes in flashes!
- I'm the Mommy! That's WHY!
- If a man yells in the woods and no woman hears him, is he still wrong?
- If Barbie is so popular, why do you have to buy her friends?
- If he asks what kind of books you like tell him that checkbooks are your preference!
- If the shoe fits... buy it in every color.
- If you have trouble getting your children's attention, just sit down and look comfortable.
- It's a shoe thing!
- Life was so much easier when our clothes didn't match and boys had cooties.
- Love is blind; marriage is a real eye-opener!
- Men make all the important decisions... Women decide what's important.
- Of course, I don't look busy; I did it right the first time!
- PMS? No, this is me everyday!
- Sometimes wild and a little crazy!
- Teach a child to be polite and courteous in the home... and when he grows up, he'll never be able to edge his car onto a freeway.

- The female's rules are subject to change at a moment's notice... NO questions asked.

- The house does not rest upon the ground, but upon a woman. - Mexican Proverb

- The main purpose of holding children's parties is to remind yourself that there are children more awful than your own.

- The sole purpose of a child's middle name is so he can tell when he's really in trouble.

- There's nothing better than a good friend, except a good friend with chocolate.

- Veni, Vedi, Visa: I came. I saw. I did a little shopping.

- What came first, the woman or the department store? Let's Go Shopping!

Women are more fun
Than a barrel of monkeys
Smarter than a wise old owl
Cuter than a wagon load of puppies
And make the best kind of pal!
- Thena Smith

What kind of friend
Tells you that you're cool
And likes the swimsuit
That you wear to the pool...
Says your kids are brilliant
And the teacher must be wrong
Loves to listen to any note
That you sing in a song...
Watches kids for you when you are ill
Or even just feeling blue
That is a special kind of friend-
A special friend like you!

Where's my Chocolate??

SPECIAL POEMS FROM LINDA

When first I heard your cry
my heart wept joyfully so,
for in that wee small voice
came a love that I would know.
You are a precious angel
sent to change my life,
to teach me about giving
and most of all sacrifice.
From that day forward
you had my heart
with a love so special
none can tear apart.
– Linda LaTourelle

Dear Daughters,

Seems like only yesterday that you were born, the memory
of that moment will forever linger on. You came to me with
divine guidance and have captured my heart forevermore.
Your beauty is beyond compare and the young women you
are becoming is such an incredible joy to watch. I remember
you as babies and wondered what you'd look like at every
stage. God has been so good to us and I am so blessed to
call you my daughters. I want you to know, I love you with
every part of my being from the beginning, and now through
eternity. Thank you for the joy you give so lovingly to me
everyday of my life. You are precious in His sight and mine.
May your life be as blessed as mine has.

Forever and Always,
Momma

In the twilight of your childhood
may the memories linger long,
to be carefree and innocent
is what will keep you young.
Don't worry over silly stuff
that doesn't mean that much,
just focus on the blessings
that are right within your touch.
Because my darling daughters
time will fly so swiftly past,
you'll wonder where it all went
and how you grew up so fast.
Your grandma used to tell me
when I was young like you,
that all the dreams I hope for
sometimes do come true.
Remember this my sweethearts
that mother loves you, too.
I pray for your success in life
knowing God will see you through.
My fervent prayer for you this year
is that you will seek His face,
for no matter where life leads you
may it be by his guiding grace.
You have always been the best in me,
I've been blessed beyond compare.
God gave to me the gift of you
and a love that is so rare.
So on this Christmas morning
will you take this gift of love,
a treasure I bestow on you
sent to me from our Father above.
– Linda LaTourelle
December 21, 2003

This poem was written for my beautiful Daughters as a gift on Christmas 2003

~

I Love You Girls With all my Heart

~

You're the Best!
~ Momma

LARA'S POEM

The sun threw itself upon your skin
The cross slit thy skin
And you seemed heavily thin
They drove thorns into your head
And blood was shed
Not for loyalty
Not for honor
But for your father
They set you up against that cross
And your back was aching
They pounded the hammer in your hands
And your eyes were of sorrow
They pounded each nail into each foot
But love was all you had to give
Everyone stood in shock and shame
Very few were in sorrow
All you had was love to give
And wanted us not to refuse
Many don't understand
Many won't
But many share your message

Written by Lara, a 14 year old home-schooled girl who has a love for writing and has been very inspired by the wonderful J.R.R. Tolkien trilogy, *The Lord of the Rings*. She is in the process of writing a book in the style of Tolkien, because of her love for his writing and her love for reading.

NICOLE'S POEMS

I love to hear the 'remember when's,'
The times we had with all our friends,
But there's one person that means the most,
The one I'd give a well-deserved toast...
She's been by my side,
And stayed in my heart,
Our friendship is strong,
And will never part.
BEST FRIENDS FOREVER

There are times that we must ask ourselves
how much do I love this person
and my answer-
words could not explain just how much

You cook-thank you. You clean-thank you
you ignore the fact that I sit on the couch
and do nothing all day-thank you
I LOVE YOU!

Have you heard? Have you heard the big news?
You're the best friend I've ever had!

Our friendship is like a song
with the perfect melody!
Thanks for always being there!

You know, eventually you stop believing in things
like Santa, the Tooth Fairy, and the Easter Bunny
but I'll never stop believing in you
You're the best friend a girl could have!

LOVE LETTERS IN THE SAND

Traditionally, love letters have always been written to your lover, husband or intended. However, love expressed in writing to those closest to us, albeit a child, parent, grandparent or even friend, is a precious gift that will last for generations to come. Love is the essence of life. God commands it and tells us to honor our husband or wife and to love our children and parents with all our heart. This section will focus on the original purpose of love letters, but please feel free to adapt the thoughts within however you feel led, for no matter who is the recipient of your writing–it is sure to be a blessing to behold.

Memories from the past, moments from the present, and dreams for the future are the ties that bind us to one another. It has been quoted that only when we give of ourselves does true love exist. So, what a beautiful gift to create as you take the time to gather treasured memories into a letter for your beloved–as a wonderful anthology of your feelings. May the thoughts within these pages be the tools to guide you gently to recall the quintessential ingredients of your love.

My prayer is that these words will inspire memories of the love that brought you together, encourage thoughts of the reasons you endure and give hope as you look to the future– for the best is yet to be. May this wisdom arouse the romantic within you and motivate you to keep the flame of love alive, not only through your writing, but each day you journey together through life.

LETTERS OF LOVE

How to Write a Love Letter

Love Letters are the epitome of romance. Whether receiving or writing, the love letter will bless. Obviously being the recipient is a delightful moment. We all have an inherent need for intimacy with our chosen. Being the author of a love letter has it's own rewards, too. It is a time to reflect on all the love you feel for this person and savor all the wonderful memories of why you fell in love.

Find a quiet, comfortable place for solitude, with a cozy place to sit. Soft music can help to clear your mind of all distractions. Be prepared with your finest paper, pen and ink, as well as a notepad to gather your thoughts and feelings. Candlelight can set a more romantic ambiance. You might like to have a favorite fragrance, too, for the finishing touch. Having a picture of your beloved near you can evoke those innermost thoughts.

Relax, remember all the special moments. Open your letter with an appropriate personal salutation, such as "Dearest ___" or "To my darling ___" or whatever you're comfortable with. Write as though you were looking into their eyes and open your heart to let the words flow onto the paper. What is it you feel, what makes the intimacy so special? Let your words enchant and impassion your beloved.

This is your time to express the most tender of sentiments. Write about the physical, emotional and spiritual qualities that are most endearing. Share your hopes and dreams for your relationship. Express your feelings as though you were the recipient. When you have lovingly professed your deepest sentiments, personalize it with a closing like "Loving you through eternity," "My heart is yours" or "I love you dearly." Be sure to check for spelling accuracy and proper grammar.

A misspelled or improperly used word will distract from the elegance of your work. Also, don't forget to sign your letter. Add some fragrance, address, stamp and seal your masterpiece. A few additional suggestions, if you have chicken scratch or the equivalent when you write, you may want to consider soliciting the help of a professional calligrapher in those times when you want that elegant touch.

The sentiments that pour from your heart into your letter will be most effective if they are easily read. Many people frame these kinds of letters, so beautiful paper, a deckle edged envelope and elegant handwriting will only add to this treasure of your love. This is a gift that will be cherished by the recipient and kept for a lifetime or longer.

Treasure the moment of your life together. Record them through the art of letter writing or scrapbooking. Perhaps share a journal together. The joy that you feel will only grow from a heart that is filled with love and passion for others. Love is to be cherished and held ever so close to your heart to be nurtured and protected. The memories of today will be a legacy for generations to come.

Your soul will shine when you write from your heart this very personal letter of love and you will see that glow reflected in the eyes of your beloved.

LOVE LETTERS

&

SWEET NOTES

The Impact of Your Writing and Why it Matters...

- ♡ To touch a heart in a special way
- ♡ To express in writing what your words cannot say
- ♡ To excite and rekindle that intimacy shared by two
- ♡ To bless and encourage someone special
- ♡ The memories of times gone by will be cherished as time fades
- ♡ To create a lasting legacy of love for many generations to come

Your Target Audience...

- ♡ Your lover, your intended, your spouse
- ♡ Your child or children
- ♡ Parents or siblings
- ♡ Special friends

The Tools of the Trade...

- ♡ Paper...romantic, elegant, masculine or feminine, fun or even funky
- ♡ The color and texture of paper...whatever suits the mood or occasion. Think Romance or Passion...the papers are endless now with the Scrapbooking craze.
- ♡ Pens...gels, calligraphy, pen and ink. For the avid writer, spoil yourself and find a selection of pens that light a spark in you.

♡ Embellishments...these really are a personal thing. The focus of the letter should be upon it's recipient and not be lost in the do-dads.

♡ K.I.S.S...My dad always told me this and this is one of those areas where "Keep It Simple" enhances your creativity.

♡ Stamps...there are always some beautiful stamps available, you must ask for them or you'll just get the mundane.

♡ Seals...visit a local stationary store or go online for seals that add that "sealed with a kiss" look as you finish your masterpiece.

♡ Fragrance is a personal touch, but for most men it can be an aphrodisiac. Try something wild if you dare or keep is soft and seductive.

♡ A dictionary...for the obvious! More about this later.

Get Comfortable...

♡ Setting up the ambience to write is as important as the pen and paper you choose. The following is a list of suggestions that will perhaps make the creative juices flow freer.

♡ Be comfortable

♡ Find a private spot

♡ Quiet, warm and cozy

♡ A comfy chair or sofa

♡ Add some candlelight with scented candles or burn incense–Aromatherapy calms.

♡ Relax a bit first, pray or meditate.

♡ Soft lighting sets a warmer tone to your thinking.

♡ Try soft music to sooth your soul and free up your thoughts.

♡ Perhaps a glass of wine or a cup of hot tea

♡ Having a picture of the recipient of your letter can help you to focus

As You Begin...

♡ Start by just writing in a random way, let your mind wander and just write as you think about your beloved. This kind of writing will loosen you up and help you to overcome writer's block.

♡ Realize that this is fun, and the end result will be a blessing for all.

♡ Remember, you're not in school and you're not being graded, you are simply sharing your thoughts and feelings by writing. It's speaking from the heart, not the mouth!

♡ Do some arm and finger exercises, neck and back stretches, sit quietly in prayer or meditation and relax. This is an exciting adventure you are about to begin!

What is the Purpose...

♡ Ask yourself why you want to write this letter. It could be for no reason at all or perhaps it marks a stage of your love or an occasion. If you have a purpose it can give a different perspective to the letter. Just a simple love letter is enough in itself and can result in a timeless treasure that will bless beyond words.

♡ As you write, focus on the recipient and as you do, make some notes as to a minimum of three qualities you love—physical, spiritual and emotional. These are the essence of who a person is because we are body, mind and spirit. Seek to express these alluring qualities as you write.

Your Style of Writing...

♡ Handwriting vs. Computer...

Would you like to open your mailbox and find love in a simple envelope? Pages of passion penned by your beloved's hand is a treasure you will cherish forever. You can almost feel their touch as your eyes read each simple word. The handwritten letter in itself expresses heartfelt sentiment simply by the act of writing.

While there are many beautiful fonts available and computers are so easy, there is nothing quite like a handwritten note. I know that personal handwriting seems to be like a big roadblock for someone's creativity, but in reality, it is and has always been truly a timeless treasure that evokes incredible memories. And to have a love letter handwritten by your beloved, oh what a delight! Even if you think your handwriting looks like chicken scratch, I can pretty much guarantee you that it will be held in high esteem forever, not only by the recipient, but generations to come.

Because of my stance on this, I will only add that computers are at best a great way to take notes, jot thoughts and do a rough draft, but ultimately there is nothing as romantic as a lover's penmanship. If you do choose to write (TYPE) on a computer, it would probably be nice to select a font that resembles a handwriting style, just to give it a more handwritten feel.

Back to School...

Here are a couple of MUST-Do's in the art of love letter writing...

♡ Absolutely utilize the dictionary...A+ spelling is a must when you write a love letter.

♡ Grammar...if you can't remember the rules you learned in English 101...get some help with a book from the library or go online. A romantic love letter is the time to brush up on your grammar skills and put your best words forward!

CHECK YOUR GRAMMAR
WiTh a
DicTioNaRy
&
ThesauRus

The Basics...

The parts of a letter...

Greeting...

How would you like to open the letter? Do you have any endearing names to which you normally address your beloved? Or would you prefer to be more romantic? The greeting can be as simple as hello, or you may elaborate and come up with something enchanting or fun. Personalize it with "Dear _____," "To my darling _____:" "My Beloved," "Sweet Sexy Sir" and so on are great salutations to begin your letter.

The Body...

The body of the letter is where you will express whatever your intentions are for this letter. You may choose to ramble and be flowery in telling of your feelings. Or you may be specific if you are writing for a particular purpose. You don't have to be Shakespeare to write the perfect love letter. All you need to know is how you feel. What makes a love letter so romantic is that it is deeply personal and it can show them how well you know them. Don't write about anyone except the two of you. Be sincere, truthful, write from the heart and they will be blessed and so will you. If you need inspiration try checking out poetry books on love from your local library or surf the net. There are many, many styles of love letters, but the one that is the best is the one you write from your heart. To help feel at ease pretend you are sitting right in front of your beloved. What are you feeling? What do you want to tell them? Start slowly and softly, the words always come when you search your heart.

The Closing...

Always conclude your letter with thoughts and hopes for the future of your relationship. These are the closing words that will be like the kiss upon their soul. Will you leave them wanting more? Will you pamper them with passion? Will you encourage and be tender with your closing? Passion, gentleness, joy, these are all symbolic of your love. When closing, you will want to sum up your feelings in a few short words that will impact the reader. "Affectionately yours," "Til we meet again," "Truly and passionately yours," "Holding you in my heart," etc.

Above all–Have fun with your writing! Remember this is a gift of you, not a contest, school lesson, competition or mere drudgery. You are writing to the person of your dreams, perhaps your soul mate. Think of the blessing you are bestowing upon them.

~ Note... Don't forget to sign your letter! And when you are finished, add a light scent, neatly fold, seal and stamp the envelope. Now it's ready to deliver, either in person, secretly or through the mail.

A Sample...

Below is a sample letter that will show you how simple it is to share your heart through simple words. The letter can be as long or as short as you like. Feel free to add quotations from others or even a love poem. You are limited only by yourself... so go for it and let the blessings begin! Happy writing!

Dearest Beloved,

I am taking this time to reflect upon the wonder of you. As I look back over our life together I can recall defining moments when our love blossomed. There have been down times when life was ho-hum and every so often there were moments when the magic was rekindled. Today is one of those days when I realized how my world has changed and been so blessed because you are in it. How often we take for granted the little things that keep us going day by day; pleasures such as a simple touch, a joyful smile, your breath upon my neck, wrapped in the *strength of your arms and the seductiveness of your body.* (physical) Today something spoke to me and I wanted to share with you my thoughts... (express what happened.)

You are the very best part of me, when I hear your voice it soothes as music to the soul. Your heart is *full of such incredible peace and joy* as you walk close beside me each day. (spirit) Being a part of your life has made me a better person. Your *constant love and abiding faith* (emotional) in me only makes me want to give you all of me.

You are... (fill in your thoughts)

We have forever and it is truly not long enough to ever give back to you what you have given to me. My heart is yours and all that I am or ever hope to be will be molded by my everlasting desire to serve you all the days of my life.

With passion right down to my soul...

Your adoring wife, lover and soul mate

WORDS TO WORK WITH

- Admire
- Adoration
- Adore
- Affectionate
- Alluring
- Ambiance
- Amore
- Amorous
- Angel
- Anxious
- Appealing
- Appetite
- Appreciate
- Ardent
- Aroma
- As one
- Aura
- Babe
- Beautiful
- Beauty
- Behold
- Beloved
- Blossoms
- Bouquet
- Breath
- Breathe
- Breathless

- Brush
- Calm
- Carefree
- Caress
- Caressing
- Caring
- Cheerful
- Cheery
- Close
- Comfort
- Comfortable
- Complete
- Comprehend
- Content
- Craving
- Crazy about
- Cuddle
- Darlin'
- Darling
- Dear
- Delirious
- Desire
- Desiring
- Desirous
- Desperate
- Devoted
- Devotion

- Discern
- Discover
- Doll
- Doting
- Dreaming
- Dreamy
- Eager
- Earnest
- Ecstasy
- Ecstatic
- Elated
- Elation
- Embrace
- Embracing
- Enamored
- Enchanting
- Endless
- Engrossed
- Enjoy
- Enthusiastic
- Erotic
- Essence
- Excited
- Exhilarated
- Experience
- Fair
- Faithful

The Ultimate Guide to the Perfect Card

- Fascinated
- Feel
- Fervent
- Festive
- Find
- Fire
- Fired-up
- Flavor
- Flirt
- Flutter
- Fond
- Fondness
- Fragrance
- Friendly
- Fury
- Generous
- Gentle
- Giving
- Gorgeous
- Grip
- Grope
- Handsome
- Happy
- Heart
- Heartfelt
- Heat
- Hilarious
- Holding

- Honey
- Hot
- Hug
- Hungry
- Impression
- Infatuated
- Innocent
- Inspect
- Inspired
- Intense
- Intrigued
- Jazzed
- Joy
- Joyful
- Jubilant
- Jubilation
- Juliet
- Kind
- Kisses
- Kissing
- Lascivious
- Lick
- Lightning
- Lips
- Love
- Love Bug
- Lovely
- Lover

- Loving
- Loyal
- Luscious
- Lust
- Lusting
- Magical
- Make Love
- Marvelous
- Massage
- Melodious
- Melody
- Memories
- Merry
- Mood
- Moon
- Mushy
- My Love
- Nibble
- Note
- Observe
- Odor
- Odorous
- Oogle
- Optimistic
- Palate
- Paradise
- Passionate
- Peaceful

348

♡ Peek
♡ Perfume
♡ Pet
♡ Pinch
♡ Playful
♡ Pleased
♡ Pleasure
♡ Privileged
♡ Punch
♡ Rainbow
♡ Rapture
♡ Rapturous
♡ Recognize
♡ Relaxed
♡ Restful
♡ Reverent
♡ Romance
♡ Romantic
♡ Romeo
♡ Rose
♡ Rub
♡ Satiny
♡ Satisfied
♡ Satisfy
♡ Savor
♡ Scent
♡ Scratch
♡ Secret

♡ Seductive
♡ Seeing
♡ Sense
♡ Sensitive
♡ Sensual
♡ Sensuality
♡ Sensuous
♡ Sentimental
♡ Serene
♡ Sex
♡ Sexy
♡ Shimmer
♡ Shine
♡ Sight
♡ Silky
♡ Sincere
♡ Smooth
♡ Soul
♡ Sparkling
♡ Spicy
♡ Spirited
♡ Squeeze
♡ Stardust
♡ Starlight
♡ Stars
♡ Stormy
♡ Stroke
♡ Surprised

♡ Sweet
♡ Sympathetic
♡ Taste
♡ Tasting
♡ Temptation
♡ Tender
♡ Tenderly
♡ Tenderness
♡ Thinking
♡ Thirst
♡ Thoughtful
♡ Thrilled
♡ Thunder
♡ Timeless
♡ Touching
♡ Unbelieving
♡ Value
♡ Velvet
♡ Vision
♡ Vivacious
♡ Voyage
♡ Warm
♡ Warmth
♡ Whisper
♡ Wild
♡ Zeal
♡ Zealous
♡ Zest

POSTAL ABBREVIATIONS

Alabama	AL	Puerto Rico	PR	
Alaska	AK	Rhode Island	RI	
American Samoa	AS	South Carolina	SC	
Arizona	AZ	Ohio	OH	
Arkansas	AR	Oklahoma	OK	
California	CA	Oregon	OR	
Colorado	CO	Palau	PW	
Connecticut	CT	South Dakota	SD	
Delaware	DE	Tennessee	TN	
District of Columbia	DC	Texas	TX	
Fed States of Micronesia	FM	Utah	UT	
Florida	FL	Vermont	VT	
Georgia	GA	Virgin Island	VI	
Hawaii	HI	Virginia	VA	
Idaho	ID	Washington	WA	
Illinois	IL	West Virginia	WV	
Indiana	IN	Wisconsin	WI	
Iowa	IA	Wyoming	WY	
Kansas	KS			
Kentucky	KY	*Canadian Abbreviations*		
Louisiana	LA	Alberta	AB	
Maine	ME	British Columbia	BC	
Marshall Islands	MH	Manitoba	MB	
Maryland	MD	New Brunswick	NB	
Massachusetts	MA	Newfoundland -Labrador	NL	
Michigan	MI	Northwest Territories	NT	
Minnesota	MN	Nova Scotia	NS	
Mississippi	MS	Ontario	ON	
Missouri	MO	Prince Edward Island	PE	
Montana	MT	Quebec	QC	
Nebraska	NE	Saskatchewan	SK	
Nevada	NV	Yukon	YT	
New Hampshire	NH	American Samoa	AS	
New Jersey	NJ	Guam	GU	
New Mexico	NM	Marshall Islands	MH	
New York	NY	Northern Mariana Islands	MP	
North Carolina	NC	Palau	PW	
North Dakota	ND	Puerto Rico	PR	
Pennsylvania	PA	Virgin Islands	VI	

HOLIDAYS BY MONTh

January
New Year's Eve
New Year's Day
Martin Luther King Jr. Day
Epiphany
Jewish New Year of the Trees
Chinese New Year
Australia Day

February
Groundhog Day
Black History Month
Mardi Gras
President's Day
Valentine's Day
Leap Year

March
Lent
Ash Wednesday
International Women's Day
St. Patrick's Day
Greek Independence Day

April
April Fool's Day
Passover
Easter
Palm Sunday
Holy Thursday
Good Friday
Easter Sunday
Arbor Day
Earth Day
St. George's Day

May
May Day
Cinco de Mayo
Memorial Day
Mother's Day
Citizenship Day - Canada
Victoria Day

June
Father's Day
Flag Day
Summer Solstice

July
Canada Day
Fourth of July

August
Hiroshima Day

September
Labor Day
National Grandparents Day
See you at the Pole
Autumn Equinox
International Day of Peace
Jewish High Holy Days
Rosh Hashanah
Yom Kippur

October
Octoberfest
Canadian Thanksgiving
Columbus Day
Halloween

November
Remembrance Day
Veteran's Day
US Thanksgiving
St. Catherine's Day
Ramadan
St. Andrew's Day

December
Advent
Chanukah
St. Nicholas Day
St. Lucia Day
Winter Solstice
Christmas Eve
Christmas Day
Boxing Day
St. Stephen's Day
Kwanzaa
Twelve Days of Christmas
Holy Innocents

BIRTHSTONES & FLOWERS

January
Garnet ~ "Constancy" ~ Carnation

February
Amethyst ~ "Sincerity" ~ Violet

March
Aquamarine ~ "Courage" ~ Daffodil

April
Diamond ~ "Innocence" ~ Sweet Pea & Daisy

May
Emerald ~ "Success" ~ Lily of the Valley

June
Pearl ~ "Health" ~ Rose

July
Ruby ~ "Contentment" ~ Larkspur

August
Peridot ~ "Happiness" ~ Poppy

September
Sapphire ~ "Clear Thinking" ~ Morning Glory

October
Opal ~ "Hope" ~ Calendula

November
Topaz ~ "Fidelity" ~ Chrysanthemum

December
Turquoise ~ "Prosperity" ~ Holly

ANNIVERSARY GIFTS

Traditional & Modern

	Traditional	Modern
1st	Paper	Clocks
2nd	Cotton	China
3rd	Leather	Crystal, Glass
4th	Linen, Silk	Electrical Appliances
5th	Wood	Silverware
6th	Iron	Wood
7th	Wool, Copper	Desk Sets
8th	Bronze	Linen, Laces
9th	Pottery, China	Leather
10th	Tin, Aluminum	Diamond Jewelry
11th	Steel	Fashion Jewelry
12th	Silk	Pearls
13th	Lace	Textiles, Furs
14th	Ivory	Gold Jewelry
15th	Crystal	Watches
20th	China	Platinum
25th	Silver	Sterling Silver
30th	Pearl	Diamond
35th	Coral	Jade
40th	Ruby	Ruby
45th	Sapphire	Sapphire
50th	Gold	Gold
55th	Emerald	Emerald
60th	Diamond	Diamond

These are ideas for wedding anniversary gifts that
may be of help when selecting a gift or
creating a card for someone special.

YOUR CALENDAR

How many times have you wanted ONE place
to keep all of your important dates?

The following pages contain
calendars for you to list the dates
most important to you!

*Plus a few pages for your
favorite poems and quotes!*

January

1_____   17_____

2_____   18_____

3_____   19_____

4_____   20_____

5_____   21_____

6_____   22_____

7_____   23_____

8_____   24_____

9_____   25_____

10_____   26_____

11_____   27_____

12_____   28_____

13_____   29_____

14_____   30_____

15_____   31_____

16_____

February

1_____   17_____

2_____   18_____

3_____   19_____

4_____   20_____

5_____   21_____

6_____   22_____

7_____   23_____

8_____   24_____

9_____   25_____

10_____   26_____

11_____   27_____

12_____   28_____

13_____   29_____

14_____

15_____

16_____

March

1_____   17_____

2_____   18_____

3_____   19_____

4_____   20_____

5_____   21_____

6_____   22_____

7_____   23_____

8_____   24_____

9_____   25_____

10_____   26_____

11_____   27_____

12_____   28_____

13_____   29_____

14_____   30_____

15_____   31_____

16_____

April

1_____

2_____

3_____

4_____

5_____

6_____

7_____

8_____

9_____

10_____

11_____

12_____

13_____

14_____

15_____

16_____

17_____

18_____

19_____

20_____

21_____

22_____

23_____

24_____

25_____

26_____

27_____

28_____

29_____

30_____

May

1_____   17_____

2_____   18_____

3_____   19_____

4_____   20_____

5_____   21_____

6_____   22_____

7_____   23_____

8_____   24_____

9_____   25_____

10_____   26_____

11_____   27_____

12_____   28_____

13_____   29_____

14_____   30_____

15_____   31_____

16_____

June

1_____   17_____

2_____   18_____

3_____   19_____

4_____   20_____

5_____   21_____

6_____   22_____

7_____   23_____

8_____   24_____

9_____   25_____

10_____   26_____

11_____   27_____

12_____   28_____

13_____   29_____

14_____   30_____

15_____

16_____

July

1_____

2_____

3_____

4_____

5_____

6_____

7_____

8_____

9_____

10_____

11_____

12_____

13_____

14_____

15_____

16_____

17_____

18_____

19_____

20_____

21_____

22_____

23_____

24_____

25_____

26_____

27_____

28_____

29_____

30_____

31_____

August

1_____   17_____

2_____   18_____

3_____   19_____

4_____   20_____

5_____   21_____

6_____   22_____

7_____   23_____

8_____   24_____

9_____   25_____

10_____   26_____

11_____   27_____

12_____   28_____

13_____   29_____

14_____   30_____

15_____   31_____

16_____

September

1_____

2_____

3_____

4_____

5_____

6_____

7_____

8_____

9_____

10_____

11_____

12_____

13_____

14_____

15_____

16_____

17_____

18_____

19_____

20_____

21_____

22_____

23_____

24_____

25_____

26_____

27_____

28_____

29_____

30_____

October

1_____

2_____

3_____

4_____

5_____

6_____

7_____

8_____

9_____

10_____

11_____

12_____

13_____

14_____

15_____

16_____

17_____

18_____

19_____

20_____

21_____

22_____

23_____

24_____

25_____

26_____

27_____

28_____

29_____

30_____

31_____

November

1_____

2_____

3_____

4_____

5_____

6_____

7_____

8_____

9_____

10_____

11_____

12_____

13_____

14_____

15_____

16_____

17_____

18_____

19_____

20_____

21_____

22_____

23_____

24_____

25_____

26_____

27_____

28_____

29_____

30_____

December

1_____

2_____

3_____

4_____

5_____

6_____

7_____

8_____

9_____

10_____

11_____

12_____

13_____

14_____

15_____

16_____

17_____

18_____

19_____

20_____

21_____

22_____

23_____

24_____

25_____

26_____

27_____

28_____

29_____

30_____

31_____

YOUR FAVORITE QUOTES

YOUR FAVORITE QUOTES

YOUR FAVORITE POEMS

YOUR FAVORITE POEMS

Thank You From Linda

The Ladies. Oh, how I am blessed to have so many special people in my life who show their love and pray for my daughters and I so faithfully. I love you all so much and thank God for the friendship we have shared over the years. Garnell, Mardell, Reba, Anna Faye, Hilda, Dorothy, Miss Mary and Caroline. Your love and prayers have carried me through some difficult times. When I have needed the warmth of a hug, the strength of a prayer, the wisdom of experience or a gentle hand to lift me up, you are a guiding light. It is my desire to share with the world that the wonder of God's love exists in the simple joys of friendship. To you my dear ladies, words do not exist that speak what my heart wants to say. You are a treasure close to my soul. Thank you for love beyond compare. I love you all so dearly.

CONTRIBUTORS TO THIS BOOK.

Jennifer Byerly

Jennifer was born in Oregon where she and her husband of 22 years reside. The couple adopted two beautiful children at birth and Jennifer counts herself as blessed to be able to stay home full time with them. Jennifer has dabbled in poetry since she was a child, but it wasn't until 2003 when her youngest daughter was diagnosed with a very perplexing and heart-breaking disorder that she really began to write. "Writing poetry has become a wonderful therapeutic outlet for me." The author credits her modest talent as a direct gift from the Lord. "I do not know how long God will place these words in my heart, but I do plan to write until He tells me I am finished." Jennifer finds herself especially inspired at the idea of placing a smile on the face of another. "It is like an Rx for my soul." If you have a special request for a poem you can reach Jennifer at jenjoy3@comcast.net.

Lottie Ann Knox

has been giving the majority of her poetry as gifts. She was born in Royston, Georgia on May 31, 1948. Using her God-given talent, she has written poetry all of her life. Her writings are inspired by her love for the Lord. Her many hobbies include: making and decorating cakes, cross-stitch, crochet, and genealogical research. Lottie is a member of The Church of Jesus Christ of Latter Day Saints who now lives in the panhandle of Florida. Readers can find more of her poetry at www.poetry.com and www.poetspassion.com.

Kerry Higgins

Kerry is from Cornwall, U.K. and moved to Somerset at a young girl. She enjoys poetry, drawing, painting, and music.

August Jones

A husband, a father, a provider for his family. August writes in his spare time. He believes all inspiration comes from God. He writes from his heart and as a testimony of God's love and grace. His greatest desire is for everyone to seek God for forgiveness accept Jesus Christ into their heart and live for Him each and everyday. August is originally from Fort Wayne, IN. He resides in Western KY with his wife and three daughters.

Sharon Ezzell

Sharon G Ezzell lives in Troutdale, Oregon, at the mouth of the beautiful scenic Columbia River Gorge, with Barry, her husband of 32 years, and her grandson, Reed, 7, whom they have adopted. They also have a 24 year old daughter who lives close by. Sharon started writing poems at the early age of 7, and had her first poem published in the school newspaper. She has been writing ever since. Along with poetry, music has always been an important part of her life. She played the piano at church for many years and accompanied the chorus while her daughter was in elementary school. Using her gifts of poetry and music helped Sharon and her husband through many trials of life. She found joy through her poetry in helping others. Her dream has always been to have a book published using some of the poems that were written with a story behind it; most of these poems Sharon refers to as 'comfort poems.' She feels blessed that God has given her these gifts and enjoys sharing them with others.

Nicole McKinney

Nicole is a classy young lady of 18! She has been writing poetry for as long as she can remember. To share her love of the arts with others, is her life's desire. She has a joyful spirit and is active in the local community theater.

⚜

Barbara Cox

My first poem wasn't written until I was in my 40's and came with the birth of my first grandson that was born a mere 1 pound 12 oz. My mother and father, my husband and home are gone but, before God called them home he blessed me with a wonderful son, two beautiful daughters and 12 grandchildren... plus, many true and loving friends... My best friend in High School calls me long distance every night to make sure that I am doing ok. To see my poetry in print has always been a dream for me... and through you, Linda, that dream has come as a Christmas present.

Todd Jones

Originally from Glasgow, Kentucky, Todd lives in Eastern Tennessee with his wife Cindy. Together they homeschool their children Will, Olivia and Garrett (well, really Cindy does, but Dad helps.) He expresses his artistic talent through graphic and structural design by day. At night, he moonlights as a wannabe bassist, playing a variety of music. In getting to know Todd, it is easy to sense his love for the Lord. He is an extremely talented man with great vision and insight, with a giving heart, too. A totally awesome dude!

Shanda Purcell

Shanda has a great love for life. She feels just as comfortable managing the business of Bluegrass Publishing as creating and designing craft projects or writing. She is truly blessed to be in an industry were she can use all her God given talents. In her own words, she says, "The craft industry is based on sharing: your ideas, designs and family, any little bit I can contribute makes me happy." Shanda lives in Western KY with her husband   Matthew and four children: Neil, Hannah, Jackson and Emma.

Thena Smith

Thena was born in a tiny farming community in western Kentucky where she remained until she married her college sweetheart in 1965. For the last 20 years she has lived in Coronado, California with her husband, Ron and her daughter, Melissa. Thena remembers writing her first poem at the age of 7 for a class Christmas project. Her mom sent it to the local newspaper and it was published. For many years, she wrote, but failed to save her writings. Finally encouraged by a friend to save her work, they presented a collage of poetry and music that was televised on a local cable station. She also co-wrote a children's musical that was presented locally. Thena has always been a scrapper. And, as the hobby began to catch on she began to share verses with others. A local on the scrapbooking message boards, Thena has written hundreds of poems to share with her friends. More of Thena's writings can be found in her two best selling books, "Where's Thena? I need a Poem about..." and "Whispers". Watch for more of Thena's works to come at www.BluegrassPublishing.com.

Note from Thena: What a surprise when Linda LaTourelle found my website a and contacted me about using some of my poetry. I was even more amazed to find out that she was from Kentucky, a few miles from where I was born and raised in Lowes, Ky. Isn't it funny that I had to move to California to meet her and she moved from California to Kentucky and ultimately met me. Amazing what a small world exists when God has a plan. Since our first lovely chat via e-mail, we are enjoying a blossoming friendship.

A note from the author: Well, what can I say, it's been over a year now and here we are "Sisters!" God has brought us a long way in a short time! I just want to let the world know (if you don't already)-Thena is a precious jewel, who shines brightly with the love of the Lord. She is awesome and I love her dearly! Be sure to check out all her books-she has the touch of the Master's hand in her writing. You will be blessed and if you share her, you will bless others. Love ya-sis!

Teri Olund

Teri was born in Louisiana, but transplanted to Texas at a very early age. With her maternal grandparent's encouragement, she began to write little limericks at the age of 10. She is married to a wonderful man, David, and has a beautiful little boy, Michael, who inspired most of the poems in this publication. Working as a Commercial Escrow Officer, Teri began scrapbooking when her dear friend, Dana, introduced her to the "art" about six years ago. That is when Teri began to blend her love of poetry with her love of telling stories through photographs. More of her poems can be found at her website: www.teribugdesigns.com.

Linda Zimmerman

Linda currently lives in Nebraska with her husband of 28 years. Including her own five children, she has been a "mother" to sixty children, as a loving foster parent. In her spare time, she works at a local gift shop; is involved in home care for the elderly; and when she isn't busy with all that, she is a Scrapbooking Diva for others! She began writing poetry for others in 2002, when she would attend crops. She also, self-published a small book of her own poems. Linda LaTourelle met her last year at a retail show they were both attending, in Chicago. It is because of the friendship that began there that we are delighted to share her poems with our readers.

To each of you, I am so blessed by your love and goodness and am honored to call you friend. I couldn't have done it without you. Thank you so much for your

ABOUT THE AUTHORS

Linda LaTourelle

Originally from California, Linda, has been writing since her childhood. In writing this book, she hopes to encourage others to create cards that will speak to the heart of family, friends, and loved ones. In her own words, "The special people in our lives will be blessed by receiving an unique sentiment with a handmade touch. I hope that through the writings of others', my own words, and scripture, this book will be a blessing to all who read and share it's words."

Linda is a single mother, of two beautiful and talented daughters and the owner of Bluegrass Publishing, Inc., a leading publisher and creator of tool books for journaling, scrapbooking, rubberstamping, cardmaking and other crafts. She truly loves the opportunity to introduce the works of other writers to her readers. Her books offer sentiments, quotes, poems, teaching and tips on a wide array of topics. Full of joy, thought, wisdom, humor, life and love, her books reach the human heart from 5 to 105. The feedback is often, "We just love to sit and read them."

Her passion for writing, publishing and sharing the Lord through it all, has enabled her to have a business that has touched lives all over the world–showing that heartfelt words can reach across oceans and continents. Look for more wonderful and insightful books to come from Linda LaTourelle. www.BluegrassPublishing.com.

CC Milam

GG is originally from a small river town in Western Ky. In her early school years, her family moved to Fort Worth, Texas. She eagerly awaited for her return to home in KY after high school. She moved in with her great Aunt Hazel who inspired so much of her life as a young child.

GG is a follower of the Lord Jesus Christ, a wife, a mother of three beautiful little girls, a homemaker, a teacher, and now, an author and editor. GG has had a passion for poetry and writing since she was very young. Being an only child, she used poetry to express her innermost feelings of sadness and joy. Today, she still expresses herself through her writings. She feels that it helps her capture a moment in time that can be remembered through words. She hopes that her writings help others to relate and feel peace, joy and comfort. These can only truly be experienced by knowing Jesus Christ as your personal Lord and Savior. Her prayer is that you will experience His abundant love and overflowing grace. Blessings to you. GG resides at her home in a small town in Western KY with her family.

Note to Linda:

Thank you for allowing me to be a part of this book from the very first printing! It has now bloomed into 200 more pages! I have found a part of me in my writings that has been lost for a while. You are a beautiful person and a delightful friend. May all who use and read this book be blessed!

LINKS TO SOME OF OUR FAVORITE SITES

◎ Be sure to visit the websites of all of our contributing writers. You can find a link to more of their sites on our website at: www.BluegrassPublishing.com.

◎ Our favorite place for fonts is ww.letteringdelights.com. Doug and his company have the greatest selection of fun, funky and fabulous fonts for all your scrapbooking and crafting needs and wants. Be sure to tell them we said, "Hello."

◎ Need a website created? Visit Holly VanDyne our great webdesigner. She is a joy to work with and will do all she can to help you develop the site that fits your needs. www.scrapbookinsights.com.

◎ For the best in rubberstamps and related products, be sure to visit Posh Impressions, the website of Dee and Warren Gruenig. They are wonderful people and have lots of info and products available. Their website is: www.PoshImpressions.com. We love them!

OUR BEST SELLERS

We have the Largest Collection of poems & quotes
created just for scrapbookers, cardmakers and crafters!

THE ULTIMATE GUIDE TO THE PERFECT WORD
(Our biggest seller—over 200,000 copies sold!)
Linda LaTourelle

THE ULTIMATE GUIDE TO CELEBRATING KIDS
(Volume 1: birth through preschool-384 pages)
Linda LaTourelle

LOVELINES WORDART CD
(artistic quotes to be used time and again)
Linda LaTourelle

WHERE'S THENA? I NEED A POEM ABOUT...
(insightful & witty poems)
Thena Smith

THE WHOLE MEGILLAH
(Poetry for the Jewish Scrapbooker & Cardmaker)
Carla Birnberg

COLOR MADE EASY
(Includes a Free Color Buddy)
(A book to simplify color for pros and beginners)
Misti Tracy

WHISPERS
(Passionate poetry and words of love...)
Thena Smith

MORE GREAT BOOKS

THE ULTIMATE GUIDE TO CELEBRATING KIDS II
(Volume 2: Elementary School-384 pages)
Linda LaTourelle

MILITARY MOMENTS
(Words to Honor Our America Heroes)
Thena Smith

C IS FOR CHRISTMAS
(Words to Decorate the Holidays)
Thena Smith

A TASTE OF PASTE
(poems for the classroom)
Thena Smith

BOARD SMARTZ
(Learning quips & bulletin board tips)
Thena Smith

WHAT CAN I SAY?
(words with an artistic flair!)
WendiSue

Coming soon...
Pimples Aren't Permanent:
A Teenage survival Guide

Watch our website for other news...

www.BluegrassPublishing.com

THE END?

Not really—
It's the beginning of
A lifetime of creating
Wonderful sentiments
For those you love.
May you be forever
Inspired!